The
ESSENTIAL
Gardening
Made Easy™

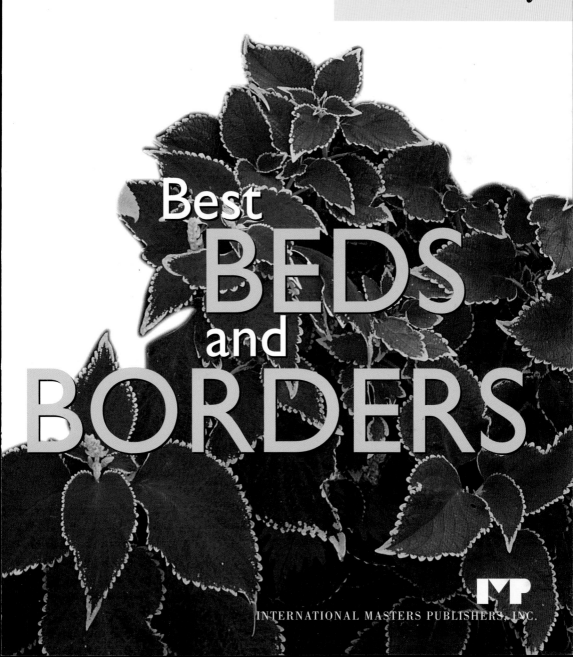

Best
BEDS
and
BORDERS

INTERNATIONAL MASTERS PUBLISHERS, INC.

CONTENTS

11 Ideas for Contrasts of
Color and Texture

15 Ideas for Creating
Bands of Color

19 Ideas for Subtle Foliage
Colors in a Border

23 Ideas for Tiers of
Pastel Hues

27 Ideas for a Rainbow-
Colored Flower Bed

31 Ideas for a Red
Summer Border

35 Ideas for a Border of
Cool-hued Perennials

41 The Basics of
Deadheading Flowers

45 A Basic Guide to
Controlling Garden
Weeds

49 A Basic Guide to
Edging a Bed

53 A Guide to Creating Island Beds in Lawns

57 A Basic Guide to Making Your Own Mulch

63 Ageratums

67 Annual Salvias

71 Artemisias

75 Bedding Begonias

79 Bellflowers

83 Coleus

87 Cosmos

91 Dusty Millers

95 Dutch Irises

99 Forget-me-nots

103 Foxgloves

107 Hostas

111 Impatiens

115 Marigolds

119 Nicotianas

123 The Essential Garden Almanac

125 Index

CONTENTS

11 Ideas for Contrasts of Color and Texture

15 Ideas for Creating Bands of Color

19 Ideas for Subtle Foliage Colors in a Border

23 Ideas for Tiers of Pastel Hues

27 Ideas for a Rainbow-Colored Flower Bed

31 Ideas for a Red Summer Border

35 Ideas for a Border of Cool-hued Perennials

41 The Basics of Deadheading Flowers

45 A Basic Guide to Controlling Garden Weeds

49 A Basic Guide to Edging a Bed

53 A Guide to Creating
Island Beds in Lawns

57 A Basic Guide to
**Making Your Own
Mulch**

63 Ageratums

67 Annual Salvias

71 Artemisias

75 Bedding Begonias

79 Bellflowers

83 Coleus

87 Cosmos

91 Dusty Millers

95 Dutch Irises

99 Forget-me-nots

103 Foxgloves

107 Hostas

111 Impatiens

115 Marigolds

119 Nicotianas

123 The Essential
Garden Almanac

125 Index

WELCOME

The ESSENTIAL
Gardening Made Easy™
Best Beds and Borders

FOR MOST OF US, "flower gardening" means beds and borders filled with continuous blooms from spring to fall. Our gardens can range in size from beds on a grand scale to small borders edging and accenting intimate spaces. Garden designs can vary from highly geometric arrangements to informal cottage gardens, or even naturalistic gardens providing transitions to wild areas. This book will provide you with many ideas about plants that complement each other in various flower garden layouts. The possibilities for beds and borders are nearly endless and should be limited only by your imagination and the plants that will grow in your region.

Flower color is probably the first thing that comes to mind when thinking about beds and borders. The "Garden Ideas & Inspiration" section provides many suggestions for coordinating colors and arranging plants in attractive, easy-care designs. You might try organizing your favorite plants into color themes: Emphasize pastel hues by using species such as sky blue Ageratums, pink Nicotianas, and mauve Impatiens, or concentrate on bold colors by filling the garden with red Petunias, bright yellow Marigolds, and multicolored Zinnias. To create a red-white-and-blue planting scheme, plant Nicotianas, Ageratums, Forget-me-nots, Bellflowers, Annual Salvias, and red or white Impatiens together in a bed. Complete information on these and other species can be found in the "Plant Guide" section of this book.

Be creative with your bed and border designs. Consider using ferns, shrubs, ornamental grasses, and dwarf conifers as background plants, and decorative herbs, fruits, and vegetables as shapely accents. Don't neglect species with small flowers but dramatic foliage like Coleus and Artemisias—they add exciting colors and textures to the garden, especially in spring and autumn when gardens need it the most. Above all, select plants that reflect your unique sense of style.

5

easy steps
to successful
beds and borders

START THE PROCESS OF PLANNING YOUR BED OR BORDER by thinking about the desired effect in the garden. Is your purpose to accent or provide color to landscape features? To provide a habitat for butterflies, hummingbirds, and other wildlife? To create a sense of privacy with a fence of garden color? Perhaps you need to soften architectural elements of your home, garage, or shed, or to create an attractive groundcover. Or, you may just want to provide a source of cut flowers. For many of us, the purpose for a garden alive with color can encompass all of the above!

Once your main objectives for designing a garden are clear, choose "the right plants for the right places." Start with your region's hardiness zone, which can be determined from the map on the front inside cover of this book. While annuals and some perennials (like Bellflowers) can be grown in all zones, other perennials, like Dutch Irises, are successful only where winters are relatively mild. Select flowers and foliage plants that will thrive in your climate. Next, determine your garden's sun and shade conditions. Shady areas are ideal for planting Impatiens, Coleus, Hostas, and Astilbes, while Salvias, Artemisias, and Marigolds do best where there is at least six hours of sunshine per day.

Soil conditions are also important for establishing successful beds and borders. Ageratums, Coleus, and Forget-me-nots flourish in moist soils that are rich in organic matter. Cosmos, Dusty Millers, and Artemisias require well-drained soil, and Marigolds and Begonias appreciate a soil that is slightly acidic. When you select plants that will grow well in the soil conditions at hand, you're practically assuring yourself a low-maintenance garden.

To prolong the blooming season, include annuals such as Impatiens, Coleus, and Begonias in your garden. These particular plants can be cared for as tender perennials by digging them up for winter and growing them indoors as houseplants.

In general, placing shorter plants in front of flower beds and taller ones at the back is a visually pleasing arrangement; it's a design that ensures all of your plants have equal access to the spotlight. Bands, drifts, and swathes of flowers are

healthy root cuttings

Mulching beds and borders not only creates an attractive background, but also conserves moisture, reduces weeds, improves drainage of clay soils, and enhances the nutrient-holding capacity of your soil. A variety of mulch materials—ranging from peat moss, pine needles, and shredded bark to plastic sheeting and stone chips—are available from local garden centers.

Alternatively, you can make your own compost or mulch at home, using leaves, plant material, and other yard wastes. The kind of mulch that you use may influence your soil. Mulching with pine needles, for example, makes soil more acidic, while using marble stone chips makes soil more alkaline. Be sure to select a mulch that suits your plants' growing needs. See pages 57-60 for further information on how to make and use your own mulch.

often more effective than a single plant.
Vertical tiers of colors can be achieved by
underplanting tall bulbs with a blanket of
low-growing Forget-me-nots or Ageratums,
or with Hostas whose foliage will cover
that of withering bulbs late in season.

Most gardeners desire colorful beds
and borders that require little in the way of
upkeep. The easiest way to reduce time
spent weeding is to pull weeds early in the
season, when they are small and before they
have flowered and produced seeds.
Mulching between your bedding plants is
another effective way to reduce weeds. In
addition to weeding, it takes just minutes to
remove withered blossoms ("deadhead") in
the garden—a technique that will keep your
plants growing vigorously and producing an
abundance of flowers.

Every few years, the perennials in
your garden may need to be rejuvenated by
dividing them while they are dormant.
These divisions can provide new plants for
other areas of your garden or wonderful
gifts for friends with gardens.

When purchasing bed and border
plants, be sure to buy vigorous, bushy ones
with dense tops and healthy leaves. Avoid
spindly plants with mildewed, yellowed, or
only a few leaves, even if they have several
flowers. Seeds are a less expensive way to
produce plants, but remember that in
regions with short growing seasons, slow-
growing species (such as Coleus) may need
to be started indoors ten weeks or more
before the last frost of the spring. Seeds of
annuals (except for hybrids) can be saved
and stored in paper envelopes or lock-top
plastic bags in a cool, dry place for
planting the next season.

a border of fiery reds

GARDEN IDEAS & INSPIRATION

Ideas for Contrasts of
Color and Texture

*To add rich visual appeal to a bed or border,
plan for contrasts between the colors, sizes,
and shapes of both flowers and foliage.*

A Garden of Contrasting Plants

To create a rich, varied pattern of colors and textures, plant bold leaves and flowers next to fine-textured ones.

Planning for contrast can add a whole new dimension to a bed or border. Even without colorful flowers, plants with lacy, fine-textured leaves are appealing and attractive when planted next to those with large, bold-textured leaves. Color also influences whether a plant has a bold or a fine texture. Bright colors, even on small flowers, generally appear to have a bold texture in gardens. Brilliantly colored leaves are also bold. Small flowers in white or pastel hues are generally fine textured. To highlight color and texture contrasts in a garden, plant clumps of plants with contrasting texture next to one another.

All the plants in this garden prefer moist, well-drained soil in sun to partial shade.

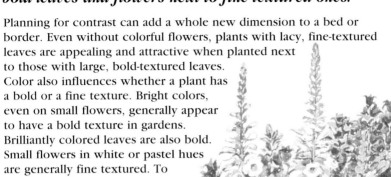

WHITE FOXGLOVE
H: 3-5 ft., S: 1-1 ½ ft.; erect spikes densely covered with tube-shaped, white flowers in early summer; large, oval leaves; biennial; zones 4-8

IRIS PALLIDA **'AUREA VARIEGATA'**
H: 2 ½-3 ft., S: 3-4 ft.; fragrant, lilac-blue flowers in early summer with yellow beards; sword-shaped leaves striped green and yellow; zones 4-8

FORGET-ME-N(
H and S: 6-8 in.; t clustered, pastel blue, white pink flowers in late spring to e summer; hairy leaves; zones

1 **Clear weeds and grass** from a 6 ft. by 10 ft. bed. Spread a 2 in. layer of rich compost over the bed and work it into the soil to 1 ft.

2 **Plant** Great Bellflowers 1 ft. from back of bed, spacing plants 2 ft. apart. Next to them, 1 ft. from back, plant Foxgloves 1 ft. apart.

3 **Group several Hostas** in a clump 1 ft. from front of bed. Space plants 3 ft. apart. Spread roots out in hole to encourage spreading.

4 **Plant Iris rhizomes** 1 ft. from front of bed. Fill in the front of bed with the Forget-me-nots, spacing plants 8 in. apart.

5 **Cut off Iris** flower stalks just above a leaf after the flowers fade. In mid-summer, cut Forget-me-not plants back to 2 in. high.

6 **In fall,** lift self-sown Foxglove seedlings with a trowel and move them to new locations, or replant 1 ft. apart to create larger clump.

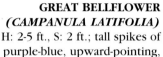

GREAT BELLFLOWER (*CAMPANULA LATIFOLIA*)
H: 2-5 ft., S: 2 ft.; tall spikes of purple-blue, upward-pointing, bell-shaped flowers from early to mid-summer; oval leaves; zones 3-7

HOSTA VENTRICOSA 'AUREO-MACULATA'
H: 2-2 ½ ft., S: 3-3 ½ ft.; spikes of violet, trumpet-shaped flowers in late summer; large, oval, green leaves with creamy yellow splotches in center; zones 3-9

•TS
ny,
or
rly
3-9

More Plants for Contrasts

TEXTURE	PLANT	DESCRIPTION
BOLD LEAVES	Globe Thistle *(far left)*	Spiny, silvery leaves; round, blue late summer flowers; 4 ft.; zones 3-8
	Hosta sieboldiana (left)	Very large, blue-green leaves; lilac summer flowers; 3 ft.; zones 3-9
	Ornamental Rhubarb	Large, deeply cut leaves; rose early summer flowers; 6 ft.; zones 5-9
	Golden Oregano	Oval, bright yellow leaves; tiny summer flowers; 3 in.; zones 4-8
FINE LEAVES	Imperata 'Red Baron' *(far left)*	Bright green and blood red leaves; does not flower; 1 ½ ft.; zones 6-9
	Artemisia 'Powis Castle' *(left)*	Mounds of lacy, silver-gray foliage; tiny summer flowers; 3 ft.; zones 5-9
	Bronze Fennel	Hair-like, red-purple leaves; yellow summer flowers; 6 ft.; zones 4-9
	Yarrow 'Summer Pastels'	Fern-like leaves; summer flowers in yellow to pink hues; 2 ft.; zones 3-8
BOLD FLOWERS	Giant Allium *(far left)*	Round, purple summer flowers; grass-like leaves; 3-5 ft.; zones 4-8
	Rudbeckia 'Goldsturm' *(left)*	Golden Daisies in summer and fall; lance-like leaves; 2 ft.; zones 3-9
	Maltese-cross	Scarlet summer flower clusters; dark green leaves; 3 ft.; zones 3-9
	Lily 'Anaconda'	Fragrant, apricot summer trumpets; narrow leaves; 6 ft.; zones 5-8
FINE FLOWERS	Snow-in-summer *(far left)*	White, star-like flowers in summer; fuzzy, gray leaves; 10 in.; zones 2-7
	Jupiter's Beard *(left)*	Fragrant, pink flowers all summer; blue-green leaves; 3 ft.; zones 4-8
	Blue Flax	Sky blue summer flowers; needle-like leaves; 1 ½ ft.; zones 4-9
	Maiden Pinks 'Microchip'	White-and-pink flowers in summer; evergreen leaves; 8 in.; zones 3-9

Ideas for Creating
Bands of Color

For a design that is stunning from any angle, and easy to plant as well, arrange flowers in ribbons of color across a bed.

A Bed of Brilliant, Contrasting Hues

Bold bands of alternating colors and flower forms, gradually increasing in height, create a dazzling effect through the summer.

This border features a simple design that yields dramatic results. Strips of colorful, densely planted Marigolds, Nicotianas, and other flowers sweep along the length of the bed. Plant height is increased gradually from front to back so all the blooms are prominently displayed. A backdrop of evergreens adds contrast and sets off the flower colors.

A design like this one is most effective on a large, sunny site that can accommodate a bed twice as long as it is wide. Plant long-blooming flowers, such as the ones in this design, to create a summer-long show.

PHLOX 'DAVID'
H: 3 ½ ft., S: 1 ft.; large clusters of fragrant, pure white flowers from mid-summer to early fall; narrow leaves with good mildew resistance; strong stems; zones 3-8

NICOTIANA 'NIKKI BRIGHT PINK'
H: 1 ½-2 ft., S: 1 ft.; trumpet-shaped, pink flowers from mid-summer to fall; pointed, oval leaves; fragrant at night; annual; all zones

COSMOS 'SENSATION MIX'

H: 4 ft., S: 1 ft.; pink, red, maroon, or white, Daisy-like flowers from mid-summer to frost; lacy leaves; plant in clumps for best effect; annual; all zones

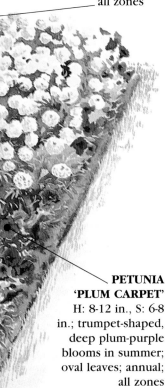

PETUNIA 'PLUM CARPET'

H: 8-12 in., S: 6-8 in.; trumpet-shaped, deep plum-purple blooms in summer; oval leaves; annual; all zones

MARIGOLD 'DISCOVERY YELLOW'

H: 12 in., S: 8-10 in.; globe-shaped, double, yellow flowers from early summer to fall; Fern-like, medium green leaves on compact plants; annual; all zones

PLANTING & AFTERCARE

1 Clear a bed that is 6 ft. wide and 12-15 ft. long. Mulch a 2 ft. wide path at the back of the planting area with wood chips for easy access.

2 Spread a 2 in. layer of compost and dig soil to 1 ft. Mark off a 2 ft. wide band at the back. Plant Phlox along this line 3 ft. apart.

3 Sow Cosmos seeds along back right of the bed. Working from the front, mark off a 2 ft. wide band and plant Nicotianas 1 ft. apart.

4 Finish planting with rows of Marigolds and Petunias at the front edge. Space Petunias 6 in. apart and Marigolds 8 in. apart.

5 Water Cosmos until seedlings appear. Pinch Marigolds and Petunias to encourage plants to branch and produce more flowers.

6 Mulch the bed when Cosmos seedlings are 4 in. tall. Cut spent flowers regularly. Use mulched path at the back to reach flowers.

More Plants for Bands of Color

COLORS	PLANT	DESCRIPTION
PURPLE & BLUE	Catmint 'Six Hills Giant' *(far left)*	Lavender-blue summer flowers; gray-green leaves; 3 ft.; zones 3-10
	Salvia 'East Friesland' *(left)*	Violet flowers from summer to fall; small leaves; 1 ½ ft.; zones 4-8
	Ageratum 'Adriatic'	Fluffy, blue flowers all summer; oval leaves; 8 in.; annual; all zones
	Balloon Flower 'Sentimental Blue'	Blue flowers from summer to fall; dark green leaves; 15 in.; zones 3-8
YELLOW	Rudbeckia 'Toto' *(far left)*	Gold summer blooms; lance-like leaves; 10 in.; annual; all zones
	Sunflower 'Teddy Bear' *(left)*	Yellow, 6 in. flowers in summer; large leaves; 2 ft.; annual; all zones
	Dahlia 'Sisa'	Yellow summer flowers; dark green leaves; 2 ft.; annual; all zones
	Digitalis lutea	Creamy yellow flowers in summer; oval leaves; 3 ft.; zones 5-9
RED & PINK	Dahlia 'Bluesette' *(far left)*	Purple-pink summer flowers; dark green leaves; 2 ft.; annual; all zones
	Hibiscus 'Disco Belle Red' *(left)*	Huge, scarlet, 9 in. summer flowers; broad leaves; 4 ft.; zones 4-9
	Maiden Pink 'Brilliancy'	Fragrant, crimson summer flowers; evergreen leaves; 6 in.; zones 3-9
	Hollyhock 'Powderpuff Mix'	Pink, white, or red summer flowers; round leaves; 5 ft.; zones 3-10
WHITE	Lavatera 'Mont Blanc' *(far left)*	White, trumpet-shaped summer flowers; oval leaves; 2 ft.; all zones
	Marigold 'Snowdrift' *(left)*	White flowers from summer to fall; lacy leaves; 2 ft.; annual; all zones
	German Statice	Tiny, white summer blooms; leathery leaves; 12-18 in.; zones 3-9
	Coneflower 'White Swan'	White summer blooms with orange centers; thin leaves; 4 ft.; zones 3-8

Ideas for Subtle
Foliage Colors in a Border

*Combine simple, complementary colors
to create a pleasing design for a garden
corner in partial shade.*

Soft Sweeps of Color

*Mix soft silvers, smoky grays, and cool greens
in dappled shade for a sophisticated border.*

Long after most flowers have faded, foliage color
continues to add interest to the garden. A soft-colored
border such as this one can provide a lush backdrop
to flowers, or offer a restful area in the cool of a
lightly shaded garden corner.

    This border should be planted in early
spring to give plants time to fill out the
design. They will provide
foliage color throughout
summer and early fall.

    Plant larger plants,
such as the Rose-of-
Sharon, first to lessen
the risk of injuring
the roots of the
smaller plants.

ROSE-OF-SHARON
H: 9-12 ft., S: 3-6 ft.;
lush, full shrub with
pale green foliage;
red, purple, or
white flowers in
mid-summer to early
fall; grows larger in
wetter climates;
prune to control
growth and
contain within
border;
zones 5-9

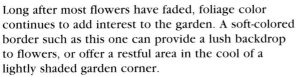

**OSTRICH
FEATHER FERN**
H: 2-6 ft., S: 2-3 ft.; graceful,
arching fronds of lacy, pale
green foliage; grows
larger in constantly
damp areas;
excellent as filler
between plants;
zones 4-8

ARTEMISIA
H: 2-4 ft., S: 2-4 ft.;
delicate, feathery foliage resembles silver
clouds; ideal complement to the coarse texture
of Lamb's-ears; mounded form can be maintained
with a light pruning in early spring; small, yellow
flowers in mid-summer; zones 4-8

FOTHERGILLA
H: 3-8 ft., S: 2-6 ft.;
simple, light green
leaves and sturdy,
brown stems on
an upright-
growing shrub;
produces white
flower spikes in
spring; zones 5-9

1 Prepare a border 5 ft. wide by 8 ft. long, digging up the soil to 1 ft. Apply a 4 in. layer of compost and balanced general fertilizer. Rake surface.

2 Position three Rose-of-Sharons 4-5 ft. apart in a triangle, with two placed close to the border's middle. Plant in holes big enough for rootballs.

3 Plant Fothergilla 2-3 ft. to right of centermost Rose-of-Sharon, closer to the front. Set rootball in the hole, slightly above ground level.

4 Plant three Artemisias along front of border 1 ft. from the lawn edge. Put Ferns to the left side, just in front of the Rose-of-Sharon.

LAMB'S-EARS
H: 10-15 in., S: to 4 ft.;
silvery leaves are thick,
fuzzy, 6 in. ovals; spreads
quickly and tolerates dry
conditions well; will not
survive harsh winter
weather; zones 4-9

5 In the front of the border, plant Lamb's-ears seedlings in holes about 8 in. apart. Plant in front of and between the Artemisias.

6 Prune Rose-of-Sharons in early spring to allow for growth of the Ferns. Prune back Lamb's-ears as they begin to encroach on the lawn.

More Plants for Foliage Color

COLORS	PLANT	DESCRIPTION
GREEN/VARIEGATED	Periwinkle *(far left)*	Shiny, green leaves; white or blue spring blooms; 5 in.; zones 4-8
	Variegated Liriope *(left)*	White- or gold-striped, narrow, green leaves; 8 in.; zones 5-9
	English Ivy	Leaves vary in shape; variegated or shades of green; 4-12 in.; zones 5-9
	Bishop's Weed	Spreading groundcover with cream-colored variegation; 6 in.; zones 4-9
BLUE/GRAY	Juniper *(far left)*	Blue-green evergreen in many textures and sizes; 2 ft.; zones 5-9
	Wild Indigo *(left)*	Blue-green foliage; will tolerate poor soils; 3-6 ft.; zones 3-10
	Hosta tokudama	Blue or variegated, shiny foliage that dies in fall; 2 ft.; zones 5-9
	Blue Fescue	Ornamental grass with thin, dusty blue blades; 8-12 in.; zones 5-9
YELLOW/GOLD	Fragrant Olive *(far left)*	Creamy yellow-variegated foliage; up to 10 ft.; zones 8-10
	Gold Dust Plant *(left)*	Dark green leaves with golden yellow patches; 6 ft.; zones 7-9
	Yellow-edged California Privet	Pale green leaves edged in yellow on bushy form; 4 ft.; zones 5-9
	Variegated Mondo Grass	Green-striped, light yellow leaves; thin, arching blades; 1 ft.; zones 5-9
RED/PINK	Carpet Bugle *(far left)*	Maroon to purple leaves; vigorous groundcover; 6-8 in.; zones 3-8
	Common Coleus *(left)*	Serrated, pink, red, and gold-green leaves; 18 in.; annual; all zones
	Tellima grandiflora	Reddish purple, deeply textured leaves; 2 ft.; zones 4-8
	Japanese Maple	Delicate, bronze-red leaves; bright red in autumn; 4 ft.; zones 5-8

Ideas for
Tiers of Pastel Hues

Add an elegant touch to a shrub border, foundation planting, or flower garden by planting an edging of soft-colored annuals in stair-stepped heights.

Rows of Blooms in Delicate Hues

Annuals come in many pastel hues and are ideal for tiered edgings because of their uniform heights and habits.

In this elegant planting, rows of closely spaced annuals become bands of color. A pastel color scheme ensures that each band blends with the next. By arranging the flowers from shortest to tallest, the color of each row is shown to advantage. A gently sloping bed emphasizes the differences in height between the plants.

This design is effective alone or used as an edging to an existing planting. Rows can run straight or curve to fit the site. All plants thrive in full sun with rich, well-drained soil.

NICOTIANA 'DOMINO WHITE'
H: 12-14 in., S: 10-12 in.; masses of elegant, pure white trumpets in summer; oval leaves on heat-tolerant, compact plants; annual; all zones

AGERATUM 'BLUE MINK'
H and S: 8-12 in.; dense clusters of woolly, button-like, lavender-blue flowers from summer to fall; medium-green leaves; annual; all zones

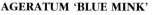

IMPATIENS 'DAZZLER ROSE'
H and S: 8 in.; mounds of single, pink flowers from early summer to frost; oval leaves; annual; all zones

CHRYSANTHEMUM MULTICAULE 'MOONLIGHT'
H: 8 in., S: 10-12 in.; lemon yellow, Daisy-like blooms in summer; narrow leaves; annual; all zones

DUSTY MILLER 'SILVER DUST'
H and S: 9 in.; foliage plant with finely cut, silver-gray to white leaves; tiny, yellow flowers in summer; remove flowers when they appear; annual; all zones

1 **Clear all weeds** and lawngrass from a 4 ft. wide site that is at least 8 ft. long. Spread 2 in. of compost and dig in to a depth of 1 ft.

2 **Use a hoe** to gently slope the soil so the back of the bed is 6 in. higher than the front. Mark five rows with string along length of bed.

3 **Plant Nicotianas** 9 in. apart along the back of the planting, 5 in. from edge. Plant Ageratums in front of Nicotianas, spaced 7 in. apart.

4 **Plant rows** of Dusty Millers, Impatiens, and *Chrysanthemum,* spacing the plants 8 in. apart. Space rows 5-6 in. apart.

5 **Pinch Dusty Millers** to encourage branching. Mulch the soil with chopped leaves and water regularly to keep it evenly moist.

6 **In fall,** pull up plants and compost them. Mulch the soil with 1 in. of compost or chopped leaves to enrich it for next spring.

More Annuals for Tiers of Pastel Hues

HEIGHT	PLANT	DESCRIPTION
EDGING PLANTS	Zinnia 'Tropic Snow' *(far left)*	White Daisies from summer to fall; narrow leaves; 8 in.; all zones
	Pansy 'Imperial Pink Shades' *(left)*	Pale and rose pink spring flowers; dark green leaves; 7 in.; all zones
	Marigold 'Antigua Primrose'	Pale yellow summer to frost flowers; Fern-like leaves; 10-12 in.; all zones
	Snapdragon 'Chimes Mix'	Pink, rose, yellow, or white spring flowers; thin leaves; 8 in.; all zones
LOW PLANTS	Petunia 'Pink Morn' *(far left)*	Pink summer trumpets with white "eyes"; oval leaves; 10 in.; all zones
	Swan River Daisy 'Blue Star' *(left)*	Blue, Daisy-like spring to summer flowers; lacy leaves; 9 in.; all zones
	Lobelia 'Blue Splash'	Lilac-and-white flowers all summer; bronze-green leaves; 9 in.; all zones
	China Aster 'Dwarf Comet'	Purple, pink, lilac, or white summer blooms; oval leaves; 8 in.; all zones
MEDIUM PLANTS	Marigold 'Lemon Gem' *(far left)*	Tiny, single, yellow summer blooms; lacy, fragrant foliage; 1 ft.; all zones
	Polka-dot Plant 'Splash Mix' *(left)*	Green leaves splashed with pink or white; tiny flowers; 10 in.; all zones
	Laurentia 'Sophia'	Star-like, blue flowers from summer to frost; lacy leaves; 1 ft.; all zones
	Baby's Breath 'Garden Bride'	Tiny, pink summer blooms in airy clouds; thin leaves; 1 ft.; all zones
TALL PLANTS	Rose Periwinkle *(far left)*	Pink or rose summer blooms; dark, glossy leaves; 20 in.; all zones
	Dahlia 'Redskin' *(left)*	Flowers all summer in several hues; bronze, oval leaves; 14 in.; all zones
	Bidens 'Golden Goddess'	Yellow, Daisy-like summer flowers; Fern-like foliage; 18 in.; all zones
	Clary Sage 'Pink Sunday'	Loose spikes of soft pink flowers; oval leaves; 20 in.; all zones

Ideas for a Rainbow-
Colored Flower Bed

Few areas in the summer garden can match the captivating color display of an annual flower bed in full bloom.

A Rich, Full Palette

Create this stunning, summer flower bed by planting clusters of powerful colors in full sun.

Annuals are flowers that bloom only one season. Planting an annual bed gives you the chance to create a unique design that you can change from year to year. Summer-blooming annuals are usually the most brilliant and long-lasting.

   Scarlet or pink flowers, such as the Zinnias, Sage, and Begonias planted in this design, offer the added bonus of attracting butterflies and hummingbirds.

MEALY-CUP SAGE
H: to 3 ft., S: 1 ft.; violet or white flower spikes; gray-green, lance-like foliage; perennial in areas with warm winters; annual; all zones

ZINNIA
H: 2-4 ft., S: 1 ft.; available in all colors except blue; many different forms, including ball-shaped and open-petaled flower heads; annual; all zones

SCARLET SAGE 'BLAZE OF FIRE'
H: 1 ft., S: 8-12 in.; bright red flowers; oval, serrated leaves; blooms last for weeks; annual; all zones

AFRICAN MARIGOLD
H: 2-3 ft., S: 18 in.;
gold, frilled flowers
that will bloom all
summer and well into
fall if planted in full
sun and well-drained
soil; good cut flower;
annual; all zones

ROSE PERIWINKLE
H: 1-2 ft., S: 2 ft.;
white blooms
with a pink flush;
glossy green foliage;
drought and heat
tolerant; may bloom
year after year in
zones 9-10;
annual;
all zones

IMPATIENS 'SCARLET FEVER'
H: 1 ft., S: 18 in.;
bright red blooms
that seem to float
above soft green
foliage; will grow
in sun or shade;
annual; all zones

BEDDING BEGONIA
H: 12 in., S: 8 in.;
clumps of red, pink, or
white flowers; round,
green, bronze or variegated
leaves; annual; all zones

PLANTING & AFTERCARE

1 Improve the soil of a 10 ft. long by 6 ft. wide bed by digging in an even layer of bone meal, well-rotted manure or compost.

2 Plant eight Mealy-cup Sage to form a gentle "S" curve through bed. Plant four African Marigolds staggered 3 ft. apart along back of bed.

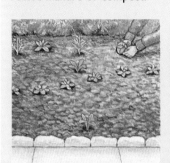

3 Place two Scarlet Sage at back center and one at the front left side. Plant white and red Begonias in the front and middle of the bed.

4 Plant yellow Zinnias at front edge of the bed, and red ones in middle among the Wax Begonias. Plant Rose Periwinkle in center of bed.

5 Plant Impatiens in the center of the border's front edge. Water the flower bed well once it is completed. Mulch with pine bark.

6 Fertilize bed every two weeks with low-nitrogen liquid fertilizer. Cut Zinnia and Marigold flowers to make them bloom more.

More Plants for Rainbow-colored Beds

TYPES	PLANT	DESCRIPTION
LOW	Sweet Alyssum (*far left*)	Ivory or red flowers from summer to fall; 3-6 in.; annual; all zones
	Campanula carpatica (*left*)	Blue or white bell-shaped flowers; toothed leaves; 3-4 in.; zones 4-7
	Virginia Stock	Fragrant, scarlet, pink, or white flowers; 8-15 in.; annual; all zones
	Livingstone Daisy	Red, yellow, pink, or ivory summer blooms; 6 in.; annual; all zones
SHORT	Globe Amaranth (*far left*)	Late summer blooms in gold, pink, or orange; 12 in.; annual; all zones
	Sweet William (*left*)	Scarlet, pink, or white blooms; 12-18 in.; annual; all zones
	Chinese Forget-me-not	Gray foliage and blue or white blooms; 18 in.; annual; all zones
	Pansy	Simple flowers in full range of colors; 6-12 in.; annual; all zones
MEDIUM	Gloriosa Daisy (*far left*)	Yellow, red-centered flowers in summer; 2 ft.; annual; all zones
	Farewell-to-spring (*left*)	Five-petaled, pink or white summer flowers; 2 ft.; annual; all zones
	Marvel-of-Peru	Fragrant, red, pink, white, or gold blooms in summer; 2-4 ft.; zone 10
	Forest-loving Geranium	Cup-shaped, violet-blue blooms in early summer; 3 ft.; zones 4-8
TALL	Larkspur (*far left*)	Flower spikes in range of colors in summer; 4 ft.; annual; all zones
	Hollyhock (*left*) (*Alcea rosea*)	Red, pink, or blue blooms in fall or summer; 6 ft.; annual; all zones
	Eremurus robustus	Pink, cup-shaped, summer blooms; needs staking; 7 ft.; zones 5-8
	Love-lies-bleeding	Tassel-like, red flowers in summer to fall; 3-8 ft.; annual; all zones

Ideas for a
Red Summer Border

Decorate a fence, foundation, or walkway with an easy-to-grow garden filled with brilliant red flowers and crimson foliage from spring to fall.

Sizzling Summer Scarlets

Make a bold garden statement that says "Welcome!" with a red carpet of annual flowers and foliage.

Use a brightly colored annual border, like this one, to give your yard an instant facelift, replace hard-to-trim grass along a fence, or even guide visitors along a pathway. Bright carpets of annual color are ideal for blocking out weeds, too.

This garden is perfect for a site that is sunny at one end and shady at the other. Mix the plants along the border, but concentrate Impatiens and Coleus at the shady end, and plant more Sages at the sunny end.

CLARY SAGE 'OXFORD BLUE'
H: 1 ½ ft., S: 1 ft.; reddish purple, heat-loving flowers; prefers sun or light shade; annual; all zones

COLEUS 'SCARLET PONCHO'
H: 1 ½ ft., S: 1 ft.; foliage plant with oval, serrated, bright red leaves; tolerates sun, but shows best color in light shade; remove flower stalks all summer; annual; all zones

**SCARLET SAGE
(*SALVIA
SPLENDENS*)**
H and S: 1 ft.; bushy
plants with oval, green
leaves and dense
spikes of red, orange,
violet, or white
flowers; thrives in sun
or light shade; annual;
all zones

1 **Dig up any weeds** on the site with a garden fork. Loosen the soil to a depth of 6 in. and spread 3 in. compost on the site.

2 **To control weeds,** spread thick sections of newspaper (8-10 sheets) out and top with pine bark mulch. Be sure sections overlap.

3 **Plant the Coleus** and Scarlet Sage at the back of bed 10-12 in. apart. To plant, poke holes through mulch and newspaper.

4 **Line front of bed** with Impatiens and Clary Sage; space 1 ft. apart. Water garden well to establish plants and then water weekly.

**IMPATIENS
'NOVETTE
SERIES'**
H and S: 6 in.;
salmon-pink flowers;
pointed, oval leaves;
tolerates sun, but best in
light to full shade; annual;
all zones

5 **Pinch off** Coleus blooms all summer to keep plants bushy. Remove faded Clary and Scarlet Sage blooms to maintain flowering.

6 **At season's end,** pull up frost-killed plants and spread 2 in. layers of compost and mulch. Next spring, plant the site without re-digging it.

IMPATIENS 'RED VELVET'
H: 1-2 ft., S: 1 ½ ft.;
bright red flowers; mound-
forming plant; tolerates sun,
but best in light to full
shade; annual; all zones

More Plants for a Red Summer Border

TYPE	PLANT	DESCRIPTION
ANNUALS	Love-lies-bleeding *(far left)*	Scarlet, tassle-like flowers; prefers sun; 3-5 ft.; annual; all zones
	Cockscomb *(left)*	Crested, velvet red flowers; prefers sun; 1-2 ft.; annual; all zones
	Zonal Geranium 'Caligula'	Clusters of crimson flowers; prefers sun; 6-8 in.; annual; all zones
	Zinnia 'Big Top Series'	Red, yellow, orange, or white flowers; prefers sun; 2 ft.; annual; all zones
PERENNIALS	Sedum 'Dragon's Blood' *(far left)*	Deep red leaves and flowers; prefers sun; 4 in.; zones 3-8
	Imperata 'Red Baron' *(left)*	Ornamental grass with blood red foliage; 1 ½ ft.; zones 6-9
	Hibiscus 'Lord Baltimore'	Red, 10 in. flowers; prefers sun or light shade; 4 ft.; zones 5-10
	Heuchera 'Pluie de Feu'	Tiny, red flower spikes; prefers sun and moist soil; 1 ½ ft.; zones 3-8
ROSES	Rose 'Blaze' *(far left)*	Semi-double, scarlet flowers; climber; prefers sun; 15 ft.; zones 5-9
	Rose 'Scarlet Meidiland' *(left)*	Shrub Rose with scarlet flowers until fall; prefers sun; 4 ft.; zones 4-9
	Rose 'The Squire'	Very fragrant, red, double flowers; prefers sun; 4 ft.; zones 5-9
	Rose 'Black Jade'	Black-red Miniature Rose; disease resistant; prefers sun; 2 ft.; zones 5-9
SHRUBS & VINES	Weigela 'Bristol Ruby' *(far left)*	Red, trumpet-shaped flowers on a shrub; prefers sun; 6-9 ft.; zones 5-8
	Scarlet Firethorn *(left)*	Shrub with red or orange-red berries through winter; 6-18 ft.; zones 6-9
	Campsis 'Crimson Trumpet'	Vine with red, trumpet-like flowers; prefers sun; 2-40 ft.; zones 5-9
	Clematis 'Niobe'	Large, ruby red blooms on a vine; prefers sun; 6-12 ft.; zones 3-9

Ideas for a Border of
Cool-hued Perennials

For a richly colored border that has a relaxing appeal, combine cool-colored perennials with blooms in blues, purples, and pinks.

Stunning, Season-long Color

With a little planning, you can plant a cool-hued border that blooms from spring to fall.

A border with a cool color scheme is ideal for adding restful appeal to any garden. Cool colors are useful for making a small space seem larger, too, since they tend to seem farther away than hot reds and oranges.

To guarantee a lustrous display from spring to fall, choose a sunny site with well-drained soil. Mix clumps of flowers that bloom in each season all along the length of the border. For a border that has lots of color at one end and not enough at the other, divide perennials and repeat clumps of the same color in several spots.

TALL BEARDED IRIS 'BLUE PANSY'
H: 2 1/2-4 ft., S: 2-5 ft.; violet-blue flowers in late spring or early summer with fuzzy, golden "beards"; blue-green, sword-shaped leaves; zones 4-8

LAMB'S-EARS
H: 6-15 in., S: 2 ft.; spikes of tiny, pinkish purple flowers in summer; woolly, silver, evergreen leaves; zones 4-9

CORAL BELLS
H: 1 1/2-2 1/2 ft., S: 1-1 1/2 ft.; airy sprays of tiny, bell-shaped flowers in pink, white, rose, or red on tall stems in early to mid-summer; low mounds of rounded, dark green leaves; zones 4-8

COMMON VALERIAN
H: 3-4 ft., S: 1 ½-3 ft.;
clusters of sweet-scented,
tiny, white to very pale
pink flowers on tall stems
in summer; ladder-like
leaves; zones 4-9

FOXGLOVE
H: 3-5 ft., S: 2 ft.;
tall spikes densely
covered with
tubular, pink, rosy
purple, or white
flowers in early
summer; rough, oval
leaves in a low
rosette; zones 4-8

**TALL BEARDED
IRIS 'SABLE'**
H: 2 ½-4 ft., S: 2-5 ft.;
rich purple flowers
in late spring or
early summer with
darker, drooping
petals and fuzzy, orange
and white "beards";
blue-green, sword-
shaped leaves; zones 4-8

**PANSY
'IMPERIAL MIX'**
H and S: 6-8 in.; white,
yellow, red, bronze, blue,
or purple, 2-5 in. flowers
with black, face-like centers;
dark green foliage; short-
lived perennial grown as
an annual; all zones

1 **Mark off a 4 ft. wide,** 10 ft. long border with stakes and string. Remove lawngrass and dig in a 2 in. layer of compost to 1 ft.

2 **Plant Bearded Irises** in late summer, spaced 3 ft. apart, with clumps at each end of the border. Plant Foxgloves 2 ft. apart at back.

3 **In spring** or late summer, plant Valerians 2 ft. apart near the back of the border. Plant Coral Bells 18 in. apart near front.

4 **Plant Lamb's-ears** 2 ft. apart at front edge of border. Fill in between clumps of perennials with Pansies spaced 8 in. apart.

5 **Replace Pansies** in early summer with later-blooming annuals in cool hues such as Mealy-cup Sages to ensure color through fall.

6 **Every three years,** dig up Iris in late summer. Discard old and diseased rhizomes; replant fat, healthy ones in a new location.

More Cool-hued Perennials for a Border

SEASON	PLANT	DESCRIPTION
SPRING	Daffodil 'Misty Glen' *(far left)*	Pure white trumpets and petals; strap-like leaves; 16 in.; zones 4-9
	Tulip 'New Design' *(left)*	Pink-and-cream flowers; white-edged leaves; 18 in.; zones 3-8
	Corydalis solida	Clustered, mauve to purple flowers; gray, lacy leaves; 5 in.; zones 5-8
	Erythronium 'Rose Queen'	Nodding, deep pink flowers; strap-like leaves; 1 ft.; zones 3-8
EARLY SUMMER	*Dicentra eximia* *(far left)*	Dusky pink flowers; blue-green, Fern-like foliage; 1 ½ ft.; zones 3-9
	Clustered Bellflower *(left)*	Clusters of violet flowers; lance-like leaves; 18 in.; zones 3-8
	Peony 'Seashell'	Fragrant, single, pink flowers; dark green leaves; 3 ft.; zones 2-8
	Blue False Indigo	Spikes of lavender-blue flowers; blue-green foliage; 4 ft.; zones 3-9
MID- TO LATE SUMMER	Musk Mallow *(far left)*	Sprays of rich, cool pink blooms; deeply cut leaves; 3 ft.; zones 4-8
	Catmint 'Six Hills Giant' *(left)*	Spikes of double, blue flowers; narrow leaves; 4 ft.; zones 5-9
	Penstemon 'Prairie Dusk'	Spikes of tubular, violet flowers; lance-like leaves; 2 ½ ft.; zones 5-9
	Aconitum henryi	Dark purple-blue flower spikes; deeply cut leaves; 5 ft.; zones 4-7
FALL	Formosan Toad Lily *(far left)*	Maroon-spotted, white flowers; leaves clasp stem; 2-3 ft.; zones 4-9
	Chrysanthemum 'Pink Ice' *(left)*	Pink late fall Daisies; silver-edged, green leaves; 15 in.; zones 5-9
	Colchicum byzantinum	Lilac to mauve flowers; pleated leaves in spring; 6 in.; zones 4-9
	Aster 'Harrison's Blue'	Lilac-blue, yellow-centered Daisies; narrow leaves; 3 ft.; zones 4-8

TASKS & TECHNIQUES

The Basics of
Deadheading Flowers

The simple task of removing flowers past their prime ensures the best blooms on your plants.

DEADHEADING ANNUALS AND PERENNIALS

YOU WILL NEED:
❑ Bucket
❑ Sharp garden shears

1 Inspect plants for faded blooms. The longer you leave flowers on the stems, the more energy the plant spends on the dying flower.

2 Pinch off blooms with your forefinger and thumb, snapping off the stem above the next flower bud. A clean break minimizes the risk of disease.

3 Use shears to cut smaller, more delicate flowers. Shears should be used for flower clusters or flowers that have fragile stems.

4 Remove dead leaves when you deadhead a flower bed. Collect all plant material in a bucket and then add it to the compost pile.

DEADHEADING FLOWERING SHRUBS

Flowering shrubs benefit from the process of deadheading. Most shrubs generally flower for one season, so removing the spent flowers will not promote new blooms that growing season. Deadheading will, however, help the shrub grow more buds and lusher foliage the following year.

Prune back stems that are carrying spent flowers. Cuts should be clean, generally above an outward-facing bud. You can also remove buds on flowering shrubs, which will encourage shrubs to grow fewer, but larger, flowers the next year. Remove a few flower buds just before the shrub begins flowering.

Leaving Only the Best

Ensure a bounty of blooms with this basic garden procedure.

WHAT IS DEADHEADING?

Deadheading is the removal of fading flowers to spur new blooms and keep a plant tidy. As a rule of thumb, if the bloom has begun to lose its color, the plant will benefit from deadheading.

WHY DEADHEAD?

For more blooms.
Flowering is how plants make their seeds. As flowers die, the plant spends its energy manufacturing seeds. By deadheading, you make the plant redirect its energy into growing blooms.

For general plant health. Flowering plants try to make seeds, especially when they lack nutrients or water. By removing flowers during dry spells, you help the plant use its resources to stay healthy.

Make deadheading part of your weekly chores in the garden

To keep beds neat. Deadheading helps keep flowering plants tidy. Dead flowers are unsightly and can ruin the appearance of an otherwise lush, colorful bed.

WHEN TO DEADHEAD

Deadhead flowers that are past their peak. The longer you leave fading flowers, the longer the plant will waste energy on dying blooms.

Deadheading should be part of your weekly garden maintenance. By checking flower beds regularly, you ensure that fading blooms are promptly removed.

HOW TO DEADHEAD

Deadheading is done in one of two ways: by cutting off fading blooms, or by pinching them off. Pinch off flowers on short stems that snap off easily, and cut off flowers on soft or sticky stems, such as Sweet Alyssum. Cut flowers on long, thick stems to just above the nearest flower bud.

Deadheading Cosmos

Pinching off a faded Petunia

Flowers that Benefit from Deadheading

TYPE	PLANT	DESCRIPTION	DEADHEADING TIPS
FLOWERS	Marigold	Blooms all summer with regular deadheading	Pinch off blooms just above the next flower bud on the stem
	Zinnia *(left)*	Pinch off blooms or cut for indoor display	Pinch off stem just above next flower bud on the stem
	Petunia	Grows bushier with regular deadheading	Pinch off stem just underneath a fading bloom
	Geranium	Must be deadheaded to maintain appearance	Deadhead at base of stem that holds spent flower clusters
SHRUBS	Rhododendron	Deadheading helps plant use energy on growth	Pinch off at joint where flower cluster joins leaf stem
	Hydrangea *(left)*	Faded blooms noticeably detract from appearance	Cut off flower clusters as they start to wilt and before they turn brown
	Azalea	Encourage next year's blooms by deadheading	Pinch off faded Azalea blooms at the base of the flower
BULBS	Tulip	For future flowering, cut before blooms fade	Cut thick Tulip stems at lowest point without cutting off foliage
	Allium *(left)*	Flowers last long before deadheading is needed	Cut stem at ground level after blooms are completely brown
	Hyacinth	Quickly becomes untidy without deadheading	Pinch off flowers at base of stem when first petals fall
	Narcissus	Can be deadheaded early for indoor display	Cut stem cleanly at base of flower with pruning shears

Seasonal Tips

EARLY SPRING
Disbudding
After last frost, but before first flowering, pinch off several buds in each cluster to encourage larger blooms.

SUMMER
Deadheading annuals
Establish a regular schedule to inspect and deadhead annuals throughout the blooming season *(right)*.

FALL
Deadheading fall bloomers
Fall flowers, such as Sedum and Chrysanthemums, should be deadheaded before the first killing frost.

A Basic Guide to
Controlling Garden Weeds

Remove unwanted garden intruders before they rob your plants of moisture and nutrients.

Weeding out the Competition

Well-timed techniques keep gardens healthy and weed-free.

WHY CONTROL WEEDS?

Besides being unattractive, weeds steal moisture, light, nutrients, and space as they compete with garden plants. This can lead to less healthy and less productive plants. Unchecked weeds also give the garden an unsightly look and detract from the landscape. In dry seasons, some weeds can even become a fire hazard.

Landscape fabrics prevent weed growth in garden beds

WHEN TO CONTROL

The best time to control weeds is while they are young and small. Weeding is much easier and more successful with small plants whose roots are not deep. Early removal reduces the chance of weeds reproducing and spreading.

Caution!

If you choose chemical controls, read product labels carefully to be sure the product is suited to the area being treated, especially if you apply the chemical anywhere near food crops.

Weeds tend to grow very fast, so frequent checks of the garden are important, starting with the first growth in spring and continuing through to the end of the growing season.

HOW TO CONTROL

Physically control weeds by hand-pulling, or dig up with hand tools, a cultivator, or hoe. Weed when ground is moist, since in hard soil the tops of weeds will break off before the roots pull free.

Chemical weed killers can be effective, but must be used with caution to avoid harming garden plants. Do not use them in vegetable, fruit, and organic gardens, unless such applications are specified on the label. If spraying, reserve the sprayer for herbicide use only.

Prevention is critical in weed control. Prevent weeds from taking root by applying landscape fabric over the soil surface. This porous material stops new seeds from taking root on top and eliminates seeds underneath from sending up leaves.

Other methods for prevention include mulching, planting groundcovers, or planting vegetables or annuals close together to limit the sunlight available to weed seedlings.

Pull weeds before seeds form

PHYSICAL WEED-CONTROL METHODS

Tip

The easiest method of weed control is hand-pulling when weeds are newly sprouted. Pull up entire plant, including roots, with a tug.

Hoeing is effective for many shallow-rooted weeds and is a simple and quick method that also aerates the soil. Hoe weekly for continued control.

A sheet of black landscape fabric can be used as a mulch to prevent weed growth. It comes in both squares that can be fit around plants and in long strips for mulching along rows of plants. Holes should be punched in the fabric to allow water to reach the soil surface below. It should be secured by placing soil or rocks along the edges.

Many hand tools will help you keep small weeds in check. These tools are designed to let you get down to the roots and pop weeds free.

For large areas, use a rototiller or power cultivator. These are good for preparing vegetable beds for planting and weeding between rows.

CHEMICAL WEED-CONTROL METHODS

Pre-emergent weed killers applied to the soil before you plant prevent weed seeds from sprouting up in your site.

Contact weed killers are sprayed directly onto leaves to kill on contact and are ideal for vigorous, growing weeds.

Systemic controls are absorbed by the weed and interrupt the metabolism to kill the weed, roots and all.

Seasonal Tips

AFTERCARE

Put your weeds to good use in the compost pile where they will decompose, naturally adding organics to the mix. In a moist and hot (over 130 degrees F. for several days) compost pile, weeds and seeds will decompose completely. If your pile is not that hot, remove seeds before composting weeds.

SPRING
Removing
Remove weeds early in the season when the plants first emerge from the ground.

SUMMER
Watching
Watch for new weeds that will sprout throughout the season. Keep them in check with physical controls, such as hoeing (*above*).

FALL
Maintaining
Continue to look for and remove weeds as you harvest your garden crops. In areas where cool-season vegetables or late flowers grow, be sure to weed beds where new, young plants are starting to grow.

Weather Watch

Avoid spraying chemical weed killers on windy days when breezes might blow the droplets onto nearby plants. Most weed sprays kill anything they touch. If you do accidentally hit a desirable plant, rinse the entire plant and surrounding soil thoroughly and immediately with water.

Once you have the weed population under control, keep things in check by applying a thick mulch to the soil surface. A 3-4 in. layer of bark chips, shredded bark, cocoa hulls, rice hulls, compost, or commercial mulch will discourage weeds and help keep the soil moist.

A Basic Guide to
Edging a Bed

Add the perfect finishing touch to a bed with attractive, easily installed edging.

EDGING A FLOWER OR SHRUB BED

YOU WILL NEED:

- ❏ Garden lime
- ❏ Square shovel
- ❏ Sand
- ❏ Rubber mallet
- ❏ 15 concrete edging
  blocks

Tip

Using large or multiple pavers, stones, flagstones, or courses of bricks allows your edging to double as a garden pathway, which is especially helpful for access between cut flower or vegetable beds.

1 Soak dry soil and spread garden lime to define where edging material will go. Curves add interest; straight lines work in formal settings.

2 Dig the trench with a straight-edged shovel, making clean, vertical cuts. Dig 2-3 in. deep and 1-2 in. wider than the edging blocks.

3 To make leveling easy, spread a 1 in. layer of coarse sand in the bottom of the trench, wet it, and tamp it down with the shovel.

4 Set the edging blocks in place, making sure they are even and butted together. Tamp them with the mallet to level them. Backfill with soil.

EDGING A BED BORDERING A LAWN

YOU WILL NEED: ❏ Stakes ❏ String ❏ Bricks ❏ Shovel ❏ Rubber mallet ❏ Sand

1 Use flat edging material you can sink to ground level, such as bricks, so the edge becomes a mow strip.

2 Use stakes and string to mark the edge, dig a trench 2 in. deeper than the bricks, and add a layer of sand.

3 Set bricks on sand at ground level, butting ends together. Level with a mallet and secure on sides with soil.

The Perfect Garden Frame

Edging adds a classic touch and provides practical benefits.

WHY EDGE?

Besides providing a natural framework to beautifully set off your garden spaces, edging keeps soil and mulch in place. It can also help direct traffic flow away from plantings, double as a pathway, effectively border a lawn by providing a mow strip, and help keep weeds from growing into your flower beds. Use edging as a design tool to create natural lines for the eye to follow or to accent bed shapes.

Brick edging helps keep a garden neat and in control

WHAT EDGING MATERIALS TO USE

There are numerous edging materials to choose from. Ready-made edging materials range from pre-formed plastic or metal strips to wired wood slats or small posts. Specially formed masonry products in cement or with rock-like finishes are designed just for edging. Wood edging includes rot-resistant bender board, straight boards, or landscape ties and timbers. Rocks, bricks, pavers, flagstones, and even logs or tree trunks can be used as edging.

HOW TO EDGE

Begin by defining your bed and marking the exact position where the edge will go. Choose edging material to fit with the design and character of your landscape. Determine a height—raised edging helps hold soil in, while flat edging is effective along a lawn as a mow strip.

Depending on the thickness of your edging and the type of construction method you choose, dig a trench to hold the material. Edging that is not properly seated will come loose and can even be damaged by equipment and traffic.

A bed of sand in the trench allows you to position the material as necessary. Anchor wood or plastic edging with stakes, and secure masonry materials with mortar, boards, or soil. Be sure the edging is straight and check your lines as you go for a clean, crisp border.

Dollar Sense

Make your own edging from wooden tree stakes. Cut stakes to various lengths and drive them vertically into soil. Or, use stakes stacked horizontally one or two high.

Rot-resistant wood edging

Edging Material Choices

TYPE	DESCRIPTION	TIPS
Concrete blocks *(left)*	Lighter and less expensive than pavers; available in many styles and sizes; easy to install	Some configured to link together for effective curved edges; set on sand
Landscape Timbers	Available in a variety of styles; redwood, cedar, or pressure-treated wood lasts the longest	Use one for short edging or stack; anchor by nailing to stakes in the ground
Pavers *(left)*	Thick, heavy, durable; available in many sizes and colors; good for curved or angled edges	All should be positioned on sand base in shallow to deep trench for installation
Cedar edging	Preformed edging made from cedar and connected by wire; available in a range of sizes	Set below ground level for holding edge; good for raised or mounded beds
Stone *(left)*	Blends with many landscapes; very durable; can be expensive; easy to install into many shapes	Position on sand in trench for stability; vary the sizes for different looks
Railroad Ties	Rustic and massive; good for large landscapes and holding back soil and slopes	Bulky and heavy, but easy to install in shallow trench; use whole or in sections
Brick *(left)*	Traditional look for formal settings; can be inexpensive; use for straight or curved edges	Mortar or install over sand; position on ends for solid edge; useful as mow strip

Seasonal Tips

SPRING

Setting out

Set out edging for new beds and gardens as soon as ground can be worked in spring. Edge beds early so everything will be in place at planting time.

SUMMER

Maintaining

Maintain edging periodically by inspecting and replacing broken or misplaced materials *(right)*. Be sure edging remains well anchored and upright.

Weather Watch

Check edging after a freeze to be sure it has not been heaved out of ground from alternate thawing and freezing. Replace after freezing weather ends.

A Guide to Creating
Island Beds in Lawns

Add interest and elegance to the landscape with a bed beautiful enough to stand alone.

CREATING AN ISLAND BED IN A LAWN

YOU WILL NEED:

❑ Hose
❑ Graph paper
❑ Shovel
❑ Organic matter
❑ Balanced fertilizer
❑ Rake
❑ Edging material
❑ Plants
❑ Mulch

1 **Evaluate your lawn** site and experiment with bed sizes and shapes, using a hose to visualize, before sketching a final choice on graph paper.

2 **Following the outline,** begin digging out the lawn area. Dig at least 6 in. deep to get most of the lawn roots. Be careful of irrigation lines.

Caution!

Be careful when you are working near in-ground sprinklers. You may need to move or adjust the sprinklers to appropriately water the new area. Use smaller sprinklers or cap the line and add a drip system to the island bed.

3 **Add new soil,** organic matter, and fertilizer to build up soil in bed. Dig this material in deeply—to at least 12 in.—and rake smooth.

4 **Border bed** with edging material for a finished look that highlights the shape. Leave 2-4 in. between lawn and edging for easier mowing.

Tip

Reduce weeding around the edge of bed by laying out landscape (weed-block) fabric over soil and under mulch. This helps keep out weeds and grass.

5 **Lay out plants** on site before planting to be sure of proper placement. Plant from the center out, putting in trees and shrubs first.

6 **Add smaller** plants, starting with perennials and groundcovers. Finish with seasonal annuals for pockets of color. Mulch entire bed.

A Beautiful Oasis in a Sea of Green

Island beds serve as accents and add color and variety.

WHAT IS AN ISLAND BED?

An island bed is a garden or continuous planting area that is bordered on all sides by other landscape elements. It is often surrounded entirely by lawn, but may also be edged with paving or seating areas. Island beds may be any size and they can include small trees, shrubs, bulbs, perennials, annuals, and groundcovers in any number of combinations.

WHY CREATE ONE?

An island bed in a lawn adds tremendous visual impact and interest to the landscape. It can be a wonderful replacement for areas of poorly growing turf and it helps reduce lawn

Island beds add visual impact to lawns and landscapes

maintenance tasks. Also, by amending the soil in the bed, you may be able to increase the range of plants that you can grow in your site.

HOW TO INSTALL AN ISLAND

Begin with a thorough evaluation of site conditions. Consider bed size and shape, sun or wind exposure, water needs, plant sizes, bloom times, and seasonal changes.

Try sketching several shapes and sizes before you decide on a final layout or select the plants. Remember that compact, sturdy, and slow-growing plants will be easiest to care for. Plan to put permanent and tall plants in the center.

Mark the area and dig out any existing lawn and weeds. Add a thick layer of organic material and more topsoil if you wish to raise

the soil level. If you want to add an edging, choose a material that fits with the surrounding landscape.

Plant the taller central plants and any permanent shrubs or small trees first, then put in perennials, bulbs, annuals, and groundcovers. Work from the center out. After planting, water everything well and add a layer of mulch over the soil.

Use a variety of plant types

Tip

Plant in drifts or masses for the most impact. Grouping plants, especially smaller ones, gives a natural and appealing look and emphasizes color and form.

Seasonal Tips

WINTER—SPRING
Planning
Plan your island bed before planting time. When weather warms, begin installation so plants will have spring and summer growing seasons.

SUMMER
Maintaining
Fertilize, mulch, deadhead, and inspect plants for pests or diseases. Water during hot, dry spells.

FALL
Preparing for winter
Slow down maintenance activities once cold weather halts growth. Remove spent annuals, replace mulch, and protect with straw after the ground freezes *(above)*.

Weather Watch

Consider installing a raised edging around the bed if soil is being washed away into the lawn. Inspect your island bed after heavy rainstorms to make sure that the soil has not washed away. Also check to see if low spots collect standing water; if so, add topsoil to make a raised bed.

AFTERCARE

Keep grass in control along the edge of the bed by trimming with an edger. If an edging material is not being used, dig a small trench around bed to keep grass roots and sprouts from spreading into bed.

Your bed will have the most impact once plants are well established. Supplement the fertilizer mixed in at planting time with regular applications of a water-soluble fertilizer. Fertilizers high in nitrogen promote green leaf growth; those high in potassium and phosphorus will aid flower and root growth. Organic fertilizers such as fish emulsion provide nutrients over a longer period.

A Basic Guide to
Making Your Own Mulch

Inexpensive, valuable, and attractive mulches are easy to make and use.

MAKING A NUTRIENT-RICH MULCH MIXTURE

YOU WILL NEED:

- ❏ Compost
- ❏ Crushed rock
- ❏ Chipper/shredder machine
- ❏ Garden debris
- ❏ Garden fork
- ❏ Shovel

Tip

Perhaps the easiest fertilizing mulch to make is compost, which you can readily create in a wire bin in the garden. Pile layers of clippings, leaves, garden debris, soil, and kitchen wastes. Keep it moist and turn it several times for quick decomposition.

1 Start with a generous pile of crumbly, dark, decomposed compost. Make your own from yard trimmings or buy packaged compost.

2 Feed garden debris— especially pruned limbs, stems, or leaves—into the chipper. Add the chopped material to your pile for bulk.

3 For extra nutrients in your mulch, add several bucketsful of crushed rock or rock phosphate to compost and chipped materials.

4 Mix together about 4 parts chipped materials, 2 parts compost, and 1 part crushed rock. Spread a 2-4 in. thick layer around plants.

MAKING SINGLE-INGREDIENT MULCHES

Make a simple, long-lasting mulch using stones. Combine small and large cobbles, or various sizes of gravel.

Dried out grass clippings mixed with peat moss (to slow decomposition) make a cheap and effective mulch.

Leaves are nature's own mulch. Rake them up after mowing, or collect them in a bagging lawnmower.

Practical and Attractive Soil Covers

Create your own mulch using common garden ingredients.

WHY MAKE MULCH?

Mulches are both easy to make and very helpful in the garden. They control weeds, conserve moisture, regulate soil temperature, insulate roots, and, in some cases, even add nutrients.

WHAT TO USE

Many materials—most of them readily available in and around the landscape—are suitable for mulches. Try compost, grass clippings, leaf mold, leaves, Pine needles (acidic), straw, crushed stone, aged manure, and sawdust or wood shavings.

Use organic ingredients for homemade mulch

Did You Know?

Sometimes, local tree and utility companies offer wood chips for free or for a nominal cost. These are the result of trimmings and pruned branches run through a powerful chipper/shredder. The material makes a very good mulch if allowed to age for a few months first.

HOW TO MAKE MULCH

Making mulch is a simple process of selecting and mixing materials. Consider the look, nutrient content, thickness, and length of time the mulch will last. Materials that break down quickly such as manure, chopped leaves, and grass clippings will need replenishing more often than wood chips, bark, or Pine needles. Chipped or shredded materials make attractive mulches that are easy to apply and last a long time in the garden.

Combining materials with good nutrient content such as compost, manure, and grass clippings will give you a mulch that also acts as a slow-release fertilizer. Inorganic mulches such as cobblestones and gravel can also be used. They contribute few if any nutrients to the soil, but they are long-lasting and attractive.

Pine needles help acidify soil

Seasonal Tips

AFTERCARE

To keep mulched surfaces looking their best and ensure even coverage, occasionally rake and redistribute mulch. Fluffing up the surface material gives it a good boost and improves appearance.

Through natural decomposition your mulch will begin to break down. Check the depth of organic mulches such as chopped leaves or grass clippings to see how they are holding up, and replenish them as necessary. Warmer, more humid climates will speed up decomposition.

SPRING
Starting
Start making and applying mulch as the garden comes to life in spring. Use a fine-textured mulch such as finished compost around newly planted seedlings.

SUMMER
Continuing
Keep making and distributing mulch as needed to keep plants cool and moist. Add garden waste and vegetable scraps to the compost pile.

FALL
Shredding
Rake up leaves (*above*) and shred with chipper or chop with lawnmower. Use as mulch or add to compost pile for next year's mixture.

Weather Watch

For protection from winter cold and wind, the usual thin layer of mulch is not sufficient. In very cold areas, apply one or more layers of evergreen boughs over tender or new plantings. Remove the boughs in spring as new shoots appear.

PLANT GUIDE

Ageratums

Compact mounds covered with fluffy blossoms

Season	*Special Features*	*Best Conditions*	
Annual	Easy to grow	All zones	
Flowers in summer and fall	Good for cutting	Full sun to partial shade	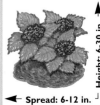
	Good for drying	Rich, moist soil	Height: 6-30 in. ◄— Spread: 6-12 in.

Powder Puff-like Flowers

Ageratums are reliable favorites for carpets of charming flowers in summer and fall.

COLORS & VARIETIES

Ageratums, or Flossflowers *(Ageratum houstonianum)*, produce dense clusters of small flowers in many shades of blue and lavender, as well as soft pink and white. They bloom reliably throughout summer until the first frost, forming lush and colorful carpets above crinkled, dark green, oval leaves.

'Adriatic Improved' Ageratum has bright, medium blue flowers on compact, 6 in. tall plants, while 8 in. 'Blue Lagoon' flowers in a clear light blue.

The **'Hawaii Hybrid'** series of Ageratums form compact, 8 in. mounds and are available in lovely shades of deep lavender, medium blue, and white.

'Pinky Improved' is an unusual Ageratum that features feathery flowers in a warm shade of dusky pink on 8 in. tall plants.

Medium blue 'Madison'

Anchoring a mixed bed

WHERE TO PLANT

Ageratums are a favorite for edgings, in beds of annuals, and in containers. They can also be used with other annuals to form plantings that make colorful patterns.

Plant low, mounding Ageratums to edge a bed of annuals. For a more natural effect, try planting groups of Ageratums so that they mingle with the other plants in the bed, rather than setting them in a straight row along the edge.

With their compact shape, Ageratums work well massed in combinations with other colorful, low-growing annuals to create fanciful patterns that look like multi-hued carpets.

Plant Ageratums to create a low-growing, soft finish around the edge of a large container or raised bed. Or, plant them around the base of a Rose bush to provide color at ground level throughout the summer.

With two colors of Marigolds a

PERFECT PARTNERS

The soft lavender, blue, white, or pink flowers of Ageratums combine well with other blossoms of almost any color or shape.

'Blue Danube' Ageratum, with medium violet-blue flowers on 8 in. tall plants, shows up beautifully when grouped with gold, yellow, or orange neighbors such as 'Lemon Gem' Marigolds or 'Dwarf Orange' Calendulas.

For a graceful, airy effect, plant 30 in. tall 'Blue Horizon' Ageratums between 'Early Wonder' Cosmos and 'Dwarf White' Snapdragons.

Unusual, bicolored 'Capri' Ageratum has clusters of blue blossoms with

dwarf evergreens

contrasting white centers
that combine well with white
Sweet Alyssums. Or, plant
them with 2 ft. tall, white
'Polaris' Shasta Daisies for a
striking effect.

Compact 'Blue Danube'

PLANTING & AFTERCARE

YOU WILL NEED: ❏ Ageratum seeds ❏ Potting soil
❏ Six-pack containers ❏ Compost ❏ Trowel

1 **Wash used containers** to prevent diseases. Fill with dampened potting soil. Plan to sow seeds six weeks before the last frost.

2 **Sow several seeds** in each cell in the six-pack. Press seeds into potting soil, but do not cover, as they need light to germinate.

3 **Keep** at 75 degrees F. Seeds will germinate in ten days. Place in a bright window and spray with lukewarm water when dry.

4 **Thin to one plant** per cell when the seedlings are 1 in. tall. Set outside to harden off after all danger of frost has passed.

5 **Before transplanting** into the garden, work plenty of compost into soil. Space smallest varieties 6 in. apart, taller ones 9-12 in.

Tip

For best growth and a long bloom season, feed Ageratums monthly with a balanced fertilizer, following label directions.

Secrets of Success

BUYING HINTS

- **Buy Ageratum** plants after the last spring frost in six-packs or 4 in. pots. They transplant easily, even when in bloom.
- **Avoid plants** with wilted leaves, a sign they may have been allowed to become too dry in the nursery.

SUN & SOIL

- **Full sun to partial** shade. Plant Ageratums in full sun except in areas with hot summers, where they do better in partial shade.
- **Rich, moist soil.** Add several inches of compost to the soil to help hold moisture around the roots.

SPECIAL ADVICE

- **Growing** up to 30 in. tall, 'Blue Horizon' Ageratum is excellent for cutting and dried flower arrangements.
- **Before the first** fall frost, dig up a few Ageratum plants and place them in pots to bring indoors for blooms until mid-winter.

 ## Seasonal Tips

 ## Plant Doctor

LATE SPRING
Direct sowing
Instead of starting seeds indoors, sow directly in the garden in a bed amended with compost and raked smooth. Thin seedlings to 4 in. apart. Plants will begin to bloom in 12-14 weeks.

SUMMER
Watering & Deadheading
Ageratums will wilt rapidly if the soil becomes dry. Consistently give at least an inch of water weekly if there is no rain. For the longest season of bloom, frequently cut or shear back spent flowers (below).

LATE FALL
Cleaning up
After the first hard frost kills Ageratum plants, pull them out and add to the compost heap. Spread a layer of mulch to protect the bare soil over winter.

Striped, green, brown, or yellow caterpillars such as corn earworms or tobacco budworms may chew holes in leaves. As soon as they appear, spray with *Bacillus thuringiensis* (Bt), a bacterium that controls caterpillars. It is available at most nurseries.

Annual Salvias

Spikes of brilliant color bloom all season

Season	Special Features	Best Conditions	
A Annual	✓ Easy to grow	⊕ All zones	
✿ Flowers from early summer until frost	✂ Good for cutting	✹ Full sun	
	⚘ Attracts wildlife	⚒ Well-drained soil	← Spread: 6-12 in. Height: 10-36 in. →

Bright Spires of Color

Annual Salvias provide a palette of radiant hues that enlivens the garden for many months.

COLORS & VARIETIES

Annual Salvias, also called Sages, are prized for their long spikes packed with brightly colored flowers, which are attractive to gardeners, hummingbirds, butterflies, and bees alike. Three main Annual Salvia species are widely available.

While Bedding or Scarlet Sage (*Salvia splendens*) is most often encountered in its fire engine red forms, it is also available in white, rose, purple, salmon, or burgundy. The colorful spikes are all offset by handsome, emerald leaves. Compact Scarlet Sage varieties, such as the crimson 'Rodeo', grow to 8 in., while others reach up to 2 ft. tall.

The 18 in. Clary Sage (*S. horminum*) has more open spikes, flowering in pink or violet-blue with interesting dark veins, like those of the 'Art Shades Series'.

Mealy-cup Sage (*S. farinacea*) blooms in white

'Flare' will ignite an entryway

and shades of blue that complement its gray-green leaves. This Salvia grows quickly to 3 ft. and is a perennial in warm climates (zones 9-11). A favorite for arrangements, Mealy-cup Sage varieties include the white-flowered 'Victoria' and indigo 'Blue Bedder'.

WHERE TO PLANT

With their long season of bloom and wide range of heights, Annual Salvias are useful in many different locations in the garden.

Plant a compact variety of Scarlet Sage along a front yard path for a cheerful welcome to your home. These bloom well in either full sun or partial shade.

Salvias in the ½-2 ft. range make excellent border plants when set in groups of

Blooming tiers of Salvias, Globe

three or five in a bed of annuals and perennials.

The taller Mealy-cup Sage looks wonderful at the back of a sunny border or edging a foundation.

Annual Salvia in a formal bed

The cool hues of Clary Sage

Amaranths, and Nicotianas

PERFECT PARTNERS

The spiked flower form and exciting range of colors make Salvias good companions for many favorite annuals, perennials, and shrubs.

The pink, purple, and blue spikes of Clary Sage 'Claryssa Series' contrast well with the round flowers of red Globe Amaranths.

Plant the red-and-white striped 'Fireworks' with white Alyssum for a burst of playful color in the garden.

Choose the violet form of the 'Cleopatra Series' to set off pink Shrub Roses perfectly. Consider planting adjoining drifts of ivory 'Alba' and 'White Porcelain' Salvias for a soothing combination.

PLANTING & AFTERCARE

YOU WILL NEED: ❏ Annual Salvia seedlings ❏ Spading fork ❏ Compost ❏ Trowel

1 After the last frost date, prepare a 6-12 in. square planting area for each Salvia plant. Fork in about 2 in. of compost.

2 Dig a planting hole for each seedling. Remove seedlings and loosen roots by gently pulling apart the bottom of the rootball.

3 Set the seedlings in the prepared holes and pat soil around the rootball. The tops of the rootballs should be even with the soil.

4 Water well. Salvias grow best if watered regularly. To avoid wasting water, install a drip system or use a soaker hose.

5 For continuous blooms all summer, feed monthly with a granular flower fertilizer. Take care not to get fertilizer on leaves.

Tip

In late fall, dig up roots of Mealy-cup Sage and store in sand in a cool place over the winter. Replant in spring for early blossoms.

Secrets of Success

BUYING HINTS

- **Buy young, sturdy** seedlings just beginning to bud. It is not necessary to buy large plants; six-packs are an economical choice.
- **Avoid overly tall** Annual Salvia seedlings reaching for light and any with faded or yellow foliage.

SUN & SOIL

- **Full sun.** Annual Salvias generally bloom best in full sun, but Bedding or Scarlet Sage (*S. splendens*) also flowers in partial shade.
- **Well-drained soil.** Add compost to enrich the soil and help hold the moisture Annual Salvias require.

SPECIAL ADVICE

- **Even if spent flower** spikes are not removed on a regular basis, Annual Salvias will continue to bloom.
- **Annual Salvias dry well** for attractive everlasting arrangements. Cut flower spikes near base and hang upside down to dry.

 ## Seasonal Tips

EARLY SPRING
Sowing
To grow your own seedlings, start eight weeks before the last frost date. Sprinkle seeds over damp potting mix in containers. Do not cover Annual Salvia seeds, as they need light to germinate.

LATE SPRING
Planting
To accustom seedlings to outdoor conditions, harden them off by setting the containers outside during the day and bringing them in at night for several days

before planting. Plant when all danger of frost is past.

LATE FALL
Cleaning up
Pull up and compost Annual Salvia plants after they have been killed by the first hard frosts of the season (*below*).

 ## Plant Doctor

Salvias are generally disease-free. If the lower leaves wilt, even though the soil is moist, the plant may have verticillium wilt. As there is no cure for this affliction, it is best to destroy the infected plants before the disease spreads.

Artemisias

Silvery foliage that lasts all season

Season	Special Features	Best Conditions	
Perennial Attractive foliage from early summer to frost	Easy to grow Drought resistant Good for cutting Good groundcover	Zones 4-10 Full sun Well-drained soil	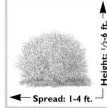 Height: 1/2-6 ft. ← Spread: 1-4 ft.

Luminescent Highlights

The striking gray leaves of Artemisias enhance the flowers and foliage of nearby plants.

COLORS & VARIETIES

Most Artemisias are grown for their feathery, silvery to gray-green, citrus-scented foliage, rather than for their flowers. These dependable plants range in size from 1 ft. tall mounds for the rock garden to 6 ft. plants for the back of the flower border.

'Silver King' Artemisia has slender, 3-4 ft. tall stems. It can spread to form a large patch. Sometimes called the "Ghost Plant", this striking Artemisia has nearly white, 2 in. long, lance-like leaves.

'Lambrook Silver' Artemisia and Southernwood form airy, 3 ft. by 3 ft., evergreen mounds of finely divided, silky leaves that are 2-5 in. long. Although the plants' yellow flowers are insignificant, the flowering stems are quite graceful.

WHERE TO PLANT

Plant Artemisias to accent perennial borders, in rock

Frothy 'Silverwood'

gardens, as a durable groundcover, or on a sunny embankment or slope.

Artemisias make an adaptable, long-lasting groundcover. Spreading by rhizomes, the metallic-hued plants tolerate dry conditions and stand up to salty winds.

Add a shimmering highlight to any rock garden with low-growing varieties of Artemisia. Provided the soil remains well drained, the unusual, silky plants will add interest to the garden for years to come.

'Silver Brocade' hides the bar

To appreciate their aromatic foliage, plant Artemisias near a path where you can brush the Lemon-scented foliage every time you pass by.

PERFECT PARTNERS

The shimmering, silvery foliage of Artemisias is as useful for softening brassy oranges and reds as it is for blending with pastel lavenders, pinks, and blues.

Plant 'Powis Castle' Artemisia, a 2 ft. tall by 3 ft. wide shrubby plant with small, finely cut leaves, to complement the purple-leaved Barberry 'Superba'.

The white, dissected leaves of Fringed Wormwood (*A. frigida*) contrast nicely with the succulent foliage of Sedum 'Autumn Joy'. Add a

Artemisias 'Silver Bouquet' in a garden

...se of 'Stella d'Oro' Daylilies

nat of gray-green Creeping Thyme for further interest.

Unlike most Artemisias, White Mugworts (_A. lactiflora_) are grown for their attractive, creamy flowers that appear on 3-6 ft. stems in late summer. They are beautiful combined with blue Asters 'Marie Ballard'.

'Powis Castle' against brick

PLANTING & AFTERCARE

YOU WILL NEED: ❏ Artemisia plant in container ❏ Shovel ❏ Compost ❏ Fine gravel

1 **Plant after last frost** in spring, or in early fall. Dig a hole slightly deeper and wider than container and add a shovelful of compost.

2 **Remove Artemisia** from container by inverting the container and tapping the rim of the pot on a hard surface.

3 **Loosen matted roots** with your fingers. Set plant in hole so that the crown sits slightly higher than the surrounding soil.

4 **Firm soil around** the rootball. Water plant well. Add a mulch of fine gravel to prevent rotting in hot, humid climates.

Dollar Sense

Propagate Artemisias from tip cuttings taken in late spring. Make cuttings about 4 in. long, trimming the base just below a node and removing lower leaves. Insert 1 in. apart in a mix of half perlite and vermiculite. As Artemisia cuttings rot if kept too moist, take care not to overwater.

Secrets of Success

BUYING HINTS

- **Buy Artemisia plants** in spring or early fall in 4 in. or gallon containers. Look for plants with vigorous, healthy leaves.
- **Avoid Artemisia plants** with wilted leaves, as well as any with signs of mildew on the foliage.

SUN & SOIL

- **Full sun.** Most Artemisias grow best and have a more silvery color in full sun. Only White Mugworts like some afternoon shade.
- **Sandy, well-drained** soil. Good drainage is essential. The stems and leaves may rot in heavy soil.

SPECIAL ADVICE

- **'Silver King' Artemisias** may spread rapidly in sandy soil in warm climates. Control roots by planting in a bottomless bucket, sunk into the garden soil.
- **Hang sprigs of aromatic** Southernwood in closets to discourage moths.

 Seasonal Tips

EARLY SPRING
Planting & Pruning
Set out new plants and prune taller, shrubby varieties, such as 'Lambrook Silver', 'Powis Castle', and Southernwood, back to 1 ft. to stimulate growth of fresh, new foliage.

SUMMER
Removing flowering stems
The flowering stems of some varieties of Artemisia may detract from the plant's beautiful, silvery foliage. Cut these stems out as soon as they appear *(right)*.

EARLY FALL
Dividing & Planting
Divide Artemisias that spread by rhizomes. Either dig up entire plant and pull apart into sections, or dig rooted sections from the outside of clump. Replant at once. Set out new plants.

 Plant Doctor

Occasionally, Artemisias are bothered by spider mites. The tiny pests, which are often red, form webs on the undersides of leaves and at the tips of stems. Control by washing away webs with a strong stream of water. Repeat if needed, as mites can be persistent.

Bedding Begonias

Easy-care beauty for shady spots

Season	Special Features	Best Conditions	
Annual	Very easy care	All zones	
Flowers from spring to first frost	Resistant to pests and disease	Shade to semi-shade	
		Slightly acidic, humus-rich soil	

eratum and Dusty Miller

Mounds of 'Rio Mix' hybrids

PLANTING & AFTERCARE

YOU WILL NEED: ❏ Begonia seedlings ❏ Garden trowel ❏ Compost ❏ Pine bark

1 After last frost, dig a hole that is large enough to accommodate the size of the rootball. Loosen soil and mix in a trowel of compost.

2 Push the seedling out of its plastic cell. Gently loosen the rootball so the roots can grow more easily. Avoid losing too much soil.

3 Plant the seedling at the same level it sat in the tray. Replace soil and pat down, ensuring the stem and roots are held firmly in place.

4 Repeat this process, planting other Begonia seedlings, 4 in. apart. Water entire bed thoroughly, and mulch with pine bark.

Dollar Sense

For more plants, cut a stem from a Begonia, strip its bottom leaves, and recut just below where leaves are attached. Dip stem in hormone rooting powder, available from nurseries, and pot indoors in damp sand. Wait three to six weeks before planting seedling outside.

A No-fuss Garden Performer

Plant compact, lush Begonias for profuse blooms that make little demand on your time or energy.

COLORS & VARIETIES

Bedding Begonias feature thick foliage dotted by abundant blooms. Also called Wax Begonias, these plants are smaller and bushier than Tuberous Begonias, which are grown from bulbs.

Dwarf varieties, such as 'Hot Tip', grow about 6-8 in. tall, and bear blooms less than 1 in. across. Averaging 10-16 in. in height, the tall varieties, such as 'Vision', offer 1 ½-2 in. wide flowers. All are prized for their vibrant hues of deep copper, salmon, mahogany, coral, or yellow.

Foliage color ranges from the glossy, light green of the 'Thousand Wonders' series, to the deep bronze of the 'Cocktail' hybrids.

WHERE TO PLANT

Begonias are adaptable plants. Although they prefer partial shade, they can bloom well in the deep shade of a tree, or in a sunny container.

'Danica Rose' in barrels

For hanging baskets, choose Begonias with bronze foliage. Varieties such as the 'Avalanche' hybrids tend to be more heat resistant.

Brighten the shade beneath the base of a tree with the dazzling red, white, or pink blooms of 'Pizzazz'. This variety does best in daytime temperatures that are below 80 degrees F.

PERFECT PARTNERS

The scintillating hues of Begonias combine well with blooms in similar, sunset shades and shade-loving foliage plants.

Begonias are often paired with the other classic shade-loving annual, Impatiens. For a great garden combination, plant hot-colored Impatiens varieties with the pink, red, or white blooms of 'Organdy'.

Splashed with magenta, red, yellow, or white, the

The fuchsia 'Richmondensis'

Begonias in a bed with purpl[...]

colorful foliage of Coleus blends perfectly with the flower colors of most Begonias, including the ligh[...] pink, deep rose, or white blooms of 'Stara'.

Marigolds are striking[...] different in shape from Begonias. Allow gold and orange Marigolds to enhanc[...] the cranberry, cherry pink, and white hues of 'Wings'.

For a cool contrast, set white-blooming 'Double Ruffles' against the shade-loving, deep green foliage o[...] Ostrich Feather Ferns.

Secrets of Success

BUYING HINTS

- **Buy seedlings** in early spring. Choose lush and compact plants with at least one seedling in bloom so you can verify the color.
- **Avoid plants** that are tall with few leaves, or those that have yellowing leaves and many flowers.

SUN & SOIL

- **Shade or semi-shade.** Begonias are able to tolerate full sun in cool (below 90 degrees F.) areas. If planted under trees, keep your Begonias well watered.
- **Rich, well-drained soil.** The soil should be kept very moist, but not soggy.

SPECIAL ADVICE

- **Begonias with bronze** or red foliage are more tolerant of full sun, and great for hanging baskets.
- **Deadheading is not** necessary because Begonias are "self-cleaners"—old blossoms are continually replaced by new ones.

 ## Seasonal Tips

 ## Plant Doctor

EARLY SPRING
Sowing
Begonia seeds are small and can be difficult to handle. Sow the seeds in pure sand.

LATE SPRING
Planting
Plant Begonia seedlings in the garden as soon as the soil has warmed. Place them outside in the daytime for about a week before planting to harden them off.

EARLY FALL
Lifting
Before the first frost, dig up

your Begonias. Replant in pots (*below*), trim the plants halfway down, and place in a sunny window indoors. These Begonias will bloom all winter and you can use them for stem cuttings in spring.

Begonias are hardy plants and remarkably free of pests and disease. Their only serious enemies are slugs and snails. Protect your Bedding Begonias with slug pellets, which are available at nurseries, or with a barrier of ashes.

Bellflowers

Best blues for summer beds and borders

Season	Special Features	Best Conditions	
Perennial	Easy to grow	Zones 3-10	
Flowers in summer	✂ Good for cutting	Full sun to partial shade	
	≈ Some varieties: good groundcovers	Rich, well-drained soil	Height: 6-48 in. ◄—Spread: 12-24 in.

Belles of the Garden

Versatile Bellflowers ring a stylish note as stately border plants or creeping edgings.

COLORS & VARIETIES

Bellflowers *(Campanula)* bloom in a range of blues, with some varieties available in white or pink. The bell- or star-shaped blossoms appear on plants that range from tall spikes to delicate miniatures.

Carpathian Bellflowers are unsurpassed for their masses of violet, cup-shaped blossoms on 12-18 in. tufts of bright green, crinkled leaves. Serbian and Dalmatian Bellflowers are 4-9 in. tall, violet or lavender spreaders.

Canterbury Bells are a favorite biennial Bellflower. They send up loose clusters of long, 1-2 in., blue, pink, or white bells on leafy, 2-4 ft. stems. The 'Calycanthema' cultivar is also called Cup and Saucer Bellflower.

The flaring blooms of Peach-leaved Bellflowers loosely cloak 2-3 ft. stems above rosettes of lance-like leaves. 'Telham Beauty' is porcelain blue. The Great

The delicate 'Telham Beauty'

Bellflower 'Macrantha' is taller, with larger and darker blue flowers.

WHERE TO PLANT

The diversity of Bellflower varieties satisfies so many gardening situations. Trail them over walls, mass them in borders and beds, or feature them in containers.

Soften edges of borders with the tidy, 6 in. mats of violet Dalmatian Bellflower 'Resholt'. Use the conical clusters of pale pink, 4 ft. Milky Bellflower 'Loddon Anna' at the back of borders.

Contour a rockery with 'Wedgewood Blue' and 'White Wedgewood' dwarf Carpathian Bellflowers, which offer upward-tilting bells on 3 in. stems. Add Serbian Bellflower 'Stella' for rich blue, star-shaped blooms that will spill over stones.

Create broad swathes of purple in borders with Clustered Bellflowers, or slip them behind Petunias in a foundation planting.

'Superba' edging a walkway

'Bluebell' and Astilbe 'Fanal'

PERFECT PARTNERS

The blue, pink, or white hue of Bellflowers lend charm to gardens large and small, informal and stately.

Punctuate cool colors of Delphiniums and Meadow Rues with purple 'Superba' Clustered Bellflower. Or use its white form, 'Crown of Snow', in an all-white evening garden with 'Miss Lingard' Phlox, Madonna Lilies, and the double bloom of Peach-leaved Bellflowers 'White Pearl'.

Add vibrant color to containers with 'Blue Clips' and 'White Clips' Bellflower Nemesia 'Blue Gem', and a mass of magenta Geraniums.

Line rows of a cutting garden with the rough-

a fence

eaved, 4 ft., violet-purple
'Brantwood' and white 'Alba'
Great Bellflowers. Or, tuck
them into the border behind
the fuller foliage of shorter
Canterbury Bells.

'Resholt' and 'Loddon Anna'

PLANTING & AFTERCARE

YOU WILL NEED: ❏ Potted Bellflower plant
❏ Digging fork ❏ Compost ❏ Trowel ❏ Bone meal

1 Remove weeds from planting area. Spread a 1-2 in. layer of compost on bed, more for heavy clay soils, and mix in thoroughly.

2 With a trowel, dig a hole slightly larger than nursery pot. Mix a handful of bone meal into soil at bottom of hole.

3 Plant Bellflowers on a cool, overcast day in spring or fall. Water before removing from pot; fill hole with water and let drain.

4 Invert container and tap to remove plant. Loosen roots and set plant in hole. Firm soil so top is mounded slightly.

5 Water after planting and weekly as needed to keep soil moist. Apply half-doses of balanced fertilizer monthly through summer.

Tip

Cut back faded blooms on Bellflowers regularly to keep plants looking tidy and to encourage repeat blooms.

Secrets of Success

BUYING HINTS

- **Buy Bellflowers** in the spring or fall. Look for healthy, full-foliaged plants without any open blooms.
- **Avoid plants that are** yellowed or wilted. Do not purchase plants with spots on either the tops or undersides of leaves.

SUN & SOIL

- **Full sun to partial** shade. Bellflowers thrive in full sun, but they require partial shade in climates with very hot summers.
- **Fertile, well-drained** soil. Enrich average soils with organic amendments, such as compost.

SPECIAL ADVICE

- **Select planting sites** where brittle stems will be protected. Locate low, spreading varieties away from foot traffic and tall varieties away from winds.
- **In summer,** support multiple, tall Bellflower stems with stakes or hoops.

Seasonal Tips

EARLY SPRING
Dividing
Divide clumps of mature Bellflowers every three to four years *(below right)*. Plant seedlings out after last frost.

SUMMER
Maintaining
Remove faded flowers. Stake taller Bellflower varieties, especially plants grown in partial shade.

EARLY FALL
Planting
Put new plants in garden well before ground freezes.

WINTER
Mulching
Cut off stems to about 6 in. before winter rains or frost. After freezing, cover crowns with evergreen boughs or straw. Remove when spring growth begins.

Plant Doctor

Septoria leaf spot fungus may cause grayish black spots on older, lower leaves of Bellflowers. Control the fungus by cleaning up affected foliage and avoiding overhead watering. In severe cases, apply a copper fungicide, available at nurseries and garden centers.

Coleus

An astonishing range of brilliant foliage colors

Season	Special Features	Best Conditions	
A Annual	✓ Easy to grow	🌐 All zones	
🌿 Attractive foliage	≈ Good groundcover	☀ Partial to full shade	
	✿ Fast growing	🌱 Moist, rich soil	

Height: 8-24 in.

◄ Spread: 8-12 in. ⌐

Fiery Color for Shade

Coleus provides a glowing carpet of fantastic foliage for shady spots.

COLORS & VARIETIES

Grown more for its exotic foliage than its flowers, Coleus gives a summer-long display of leaves in solid pink, red, orange, brown, green, white, or yellow, as well as striking combinations of up to four of those colors.

The 15-20 in. tall 'Rainbow Series' and the 10 in. 'Wizard Series' have boldly patterned, 4 in. long, heart-shaped leaves in the full range of Coleus colors.

'Saber' Coleus are dwarf, 8 in. tall plants with long, narrow, deeply cut leaves, while the 'Fiji Series' features leaves with unusual, fringed edges outlined in vibrant and contrasting colors. Colors for both types span the entire Coleus color range.

A mass of 'Scarlet Poncho'

WHERE TO PLANT

The brightly colored leaves of Coleus bring a riot of

'Golden Bedder' with Phlox

splashed color to shaded beds, borders, or containers.

Plant 8-10 in. 'Fairway' Coleus to edge a bed of taller annuals. Available in solid and mixed shades of deep red, bronze, yellow, or rose, this low-growing Coleus has smaller leaves than most other varieties.

For an Oriental carpet effect under trees or shrubs, mass mixed colors of Coleus 'Carefree', whose Oak-like, scalloped leaves have contrasting outlines.

Mass several plants of 'Scarlet Poncho' Coleus, a cascading variety whose scarlet leaves are outlined in chartreuse, for an eye-catching hanging basket or container in a shady site.

PERFECT PARTNERS

The complex patterns and bright colors of Coleus perk up many plant combinations. For special effects, look for Coleus varieties in separate colors rather than mixes.

'Queen Victoria' glows agains

Pure red 'Velvet', one of the colors in the 'Seven Dwarfs Series', makes a pleasing companion for white-and-green *Lamium maculatum* 'White Nancy'.

Mingle the mixture of bright pinks, reds, greens, and yellows found in *Coleu*

A mixed bed of Coleus benea

Japanese Barberry

blumei with white- or pink-flowered Impatiens for a long-lasting, colorful combination in the shade.

Brighten the solid green background of Ferns with an edging of 'Fashion Parade Mix', a blend of several dwarf varieties of Coleus.

espaliered Blue Spruce

PLANTING & AFTERCARE

YOU WILL NEED: ❑ Coleus seeds ❑ Potting soil ❑ Planting flat ❑ 2 ft. by 4 ft. board ❑ Plastic wrap

1 Sow Coleus seeds ten weeks before last frost. Fill a clean flat with damp potting soil and firm gently with a 2 ft. by 4 ft. board.

2 Scatter seeds evenly over the potting soil. Gently press into the soil, but do not bury, as the seeds need light to germinate.

3 To keep soil moist, but still let light in, cover flat with a piece of plastic wrap. Place in a warm, brightly lit spot out of direct sunlight.

4 Seedlings should emerge in a week. Place the flat in a sunny window. Water with lukewarm water from a spray bottle.

5 When the second set of leaves appears, transplant seedlings into individual pots. Keep in sunny window and fertilize weekly.

Tip

When seedlings are 6 in. tall, pinch tip to force side branching. When branches are 6 in., pinch to make plants full.

Secrets of Success

BUYING HINTS

- **Buy Coleus plants** in early spring. Look for compact plants that have many side branches in six-packs or 4 in. pots.
- **Avoid leggy plants** with only one main stem, and any that are wilted or that are already flowering.

SUN & SOIL

- **Partial to full shade.** In cool climates, Coleus can tolerate more sun, but they will need extra water.
- **Moist, rich soil.** Add humus in the form of compost or leaf mold to help hold moisture and enrich the soil.

SPECIAL ADVICE

- **Unless you want** to collect seeds, remove Coleus flowers to encourage better leaf growth.
- **Pot up selected Coleus** in fall to grow indoors over winter. Cut back halfway several weeks in advance to force new growth.

 Seasonal Tips

LATE SPRING
Planting
After danger of frost, set out Coleus seedlings, spacing them 8-12 in. apart. Dig in several inches of compost and mulch the plants to keep them moist.

SUMMER
Fertilizing
Feed Coleus plants every few weeks with a fertilizer high in nitrogen, closely following the directions on the label. Water plants when the top inch of soil feels dry to the touch.

FALL
Rooting cuttings
To grow new plants for next year's garden, root Coleus cuttings in a glass of water *(below)*. Change the water once a week to prevent the buildup of bacteria. Pot up when roots have formed.

 Plant Doctor

Snails and slugs can easily devour your Coleus transplants in one night. Protect young plants by encircling them with a thick ring of wood ashes or diatomaceous earth. Both of these substances deter the pests by causing irritations to their skin.

Cosmos

Paper-fine blooms in vivid summer hues

Season	Special Features	Best Conditions	
A Annual	✓ Easy to grow	🌐 All zones	Height: 1-6 ft.
✻ Flowers in summer and early autumn	✂ Good for cutting	✹ Full sun	
❄ Repeat blooms	🐝 Attracts wildlife	🛠 Well-drained soil	←Spread: 12-36 in.

Silken Saucers of Bloom

The nostalgic pastels and rich magenta reds of Cosmos flutter on feathery stems.

COLORS & VARIETIES

Cosmos brighten gardens from early summer until frost with flat, Daisy-like blooms, in hues ranging from cool rose to hot orange, above lacy, Fern-like foliage.

Delicate pink, white, lilac, or magenta blooms of the most common species, *Cosmos bipinnatus,* grow 2-6 ft. tall on open-branching plants. The popular variety 'Sensation' produces 3-4 in., crimson, rose, or white blossoms on 3-4 ft. plants. Dwarf 'Sonata Mixed' Cosmos bloom early, with 2-3 in., dark rose, pink, white, or bicolored flowers on 2 ft. plants.

For an electric display, plant Yellow Cosmos *(C. sulphureus)*. This 2-4 ft., bushy species bears Marigold-like foliage. The aptly named 'Bright Lights' offers vivid red, orange, or yellow, semi-double flowers.

The unusual, 2-3 ft. Chocolate Cosmos *(C.*

Cosmos with Marigolds

atrosanguineus) grows as a perennial in warm climates and produces 2-3 in., deep burgundy flowers that emit the scent of chocolate.

WHERE TO PLANT

Cosmos flourish in full sun even with some neglect, enjoying dry, crowded conditions. Their open form looks best massed in the back of the border or clustered in containers.

Group pots of snow white 'Sonata White' and the sizzling red 'Dazzler' on decks or patios in front of taller foliage plants. Edge the base of each pot with low-growing annuals in complementary colors.

Plant 'Sunny Red', with its scarlet flowers that fade to orange, at the corner of a garden nook covered with deep green, climbing vines. Or, fill the nook with the blushing 'Pinkie' and the vigorous, dark-eyed, pink 'Versailles Tetra' with native

A bed with Chocolate Cosmos

Vibrant 'Bright Lights' and Ca

wildflowers for a well-contained, but light and breezy-looking, meadow.

Tuck 3 ft. varieties, such as white 'Daydream', which needs no deadheading, into perennial borders to fill gaps left by erect Foxgloves and dense and upright Larkspurs

PERFECT PARTNERS

The varied shades of Cosmos create a tapestry of bobbing color in any planting.

Plant the white 'Purity'. with its bright yellow center as a snowy counterpoint to the subtle autumn hues of Maples or the rich greens of Juniper and Yew.

Focus attention on an autumn scene of New England Asters, pink Dahlias and Sedum 'Brilliant' with

...ulas bordering a fence

Candystripe', whose
...ensational, white-edged,
...ilken petals are brushed
...with shades of crimson.

Mix the unusual, tubular
...etals and Fern-like foliage of
...nagenta 'Sea Shells' with
...ale blue Scabious and
Cornflowers in a cottage
...arden, or pot them with
...railing Lobelias and purple
...alvias for a colorful effect.

rose-pink 'Sensation'

PLANTING & AFTERCARE

YOU WILL NEED: ❑ Cosmos seeds ❑ Hoe ❑ Rake
❑ Compost for heavy soils ❑ Mesh bag ❑ Scissors

1 In spring, clear planting area of weeds. Add compost to site only if soil is heavy clay or compacted and drainage is poor.

2 Loosen soil with hoe and break up any large clumps of dirt. Rake the surface smooth and remove all but very small stones.

3 Plant Cosmos seeds 1 in. apart, 1/8 in. deep, in rows 18 in. apart for a cutting garden. Make rows wavy for a meadow look.

4 Fill a mesh bag with potting soil and sand and use bag to sprinkle 1/4 in. of soil over seeds. Firm site with back of hoe. Water.

5 When seedlings are 3 in. tall, thin to 12 in. apart with scissors. Stake tall-growing varieties before they reach 12 in.

Tip

Pinch the growing tips of Cosmos plants when they reach 18 in. to encourage low branching and more flowers.

Secrets of Success

BUYING HINTS

- **Buy seeds** from seed catalogs in late winter. If buying seedlings, look for small, well-proportioned plants in good health.
- **Avoid buying nursery** seedlings without labels or tall, leggy, unbranched plants already in bloom.

SUN & SOIL

- **Full sun.** Cosmos provide months of profuse blooms when planted in full sun. Shady sites will yield more foliage and fewer blossoms.
- **Well-drained soil.** Plants will thrive in average or even poor soils, but will not survive in wet conditions.

SPECIAL ADVICE

- **Provide protection** from wind damage by planting on the sheltered side of fences, buildings, or shrubs.
- **Although Cosmos** can be transplanted into the garden as seedlings, plants will be healthier and bloom earlier if sown directly.

 Seasonal Tips

LATE SPRING
Planting
Sow Cosmos seeds after last frost in an area with well-drained soil. Set out nursery seedlings, crowding plants to provide support. Pinch growing tips to encourage new growth.

SUMMER
Maintaining
Deadhead faded blossoms to encourage more blooms throughout the summer. Cosmos not planted in large groups may require staking for added support.

FALL
Shearing
After the first hard frost has killed Cosmos plants, cut off stems at ground level (*below*) and remove to compost pile. Leave the plant roots undisturbed to provide nutrients for soil organisms.

 *Plant Doctor*

Cosmos are sometimes bothered by Japanese beetles in mid-summer. The 1/2 in., copper-colored pests eat plant leaves and occasionally flower petals. Control by handpicking pests and dropping into a jar of gasoline or kerosene.

Dusty Millers

Soft and silvery foliage lights up the garden

Season	*Special Features*	*Best Conditions*	
Annual	Easy to grow	All zones	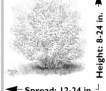
Blooms in summer	Drought resistant	Full sun	Height: 8-24 in.
	Evergreen	Well-drained soil	Spread: 12-24 in.

Delicate, Lacy Leaves

Dusty Miller adds shimmering silver hues and velvety texture to sunny areas.

COLORS & VARIETIES

Prized for their unique foliage, the various silver and gray evergreen sub-shrubs known as Dusty Millers are easily recognized by their oval, lobed, fuzzy leaves. All varieties produce tiny, white or yellow summer blooms.

One of the most popular Dusty Millers, 'Silver Dust', grows into a mound 8-12 in. tall and wide with woolly, silvery white, lobed leaves. Small, yellow, Daisy-like blooms emerge in summer. Though generally grown as an annual, this plant may overwinter in zones 8-11.

The Dusty Miller variety 'Silver Feather', also called 'Silver Lace', has finely cut, pale gray leaves. In mild climates, 'Silver Lace' also lives over the winter, growing into a 2-3 ft. plant and producing sprays of white flowers.

The lovely 'Silver Lace'

'Cirrus' edging a patio

WHERE TO PLANT

Tolerant of drought and heat, Dusty Millers look best and grow best in sunny, open locations in the garden.

Plant compact, 8 in. tall 'Silver Queen' as an edging near a path. Its pale foliage is striking at night, reflecting moonlight or outdoor lighting. On rainy days, the delicate, fuzzy leaves capture and display each raindrop.

Weave drifts of 'Cirrus', a broad-leaved variety of Dusty Miller, through a rock garden or border of low plants to create a river of solid silver-gray.

Dusty Millers are excellent for containers. Unlike plants grown for their flowers, which are often effective for only a few weeks, the foliage of Dusty Millers remains attractive and interesting all season.

'Silver Dust' with Salvia, Foun

PERFECT PARTNERS

The soft, ever-gray foliage of Dusty Millers harmonizes especially well with flowers in hues of blue, red, soft pink, cream, or white.

Plant a swathe of 'Silver Filigree', a variety with very finely cut, gray-white foliage to set off a planting of mixed 'Blue Bedder' and 'White Porcelain' Mealy-cup Sages.

'New Look' has especially large, silver-white leaves that make it an elegant addition to an all-white garden planted with Impatiens, Nicotianas, and Cleomes.

In a large tub, surround several plants of 'White

Grass, and Marigolds

Diamond' Dusty Miller with pastel pink 'Chiffon Morn' Petunias and trailing 'Carpet of Snow' Sweet Alyssum.

Dusty Miller with Petunias

PLANTING & AFTERCARE

YOU WILL NEED: ❑ Six-pack of Dusty Millers ❑ Compost ❑ Spading fork ❑ Trowel

1 After the last frost, use a spading fork to loosen the soil in the planting area to a depth of 8 in. Work in 2-3 in. of compost.

2 Dig holes as deep as the six-pack and 2 in. wider than the cell for each plant. Make a small cone of soil in each hole.

3 Working one at a time so roots will not dry out, remove plants from the six-pack. Loosen matted roots with fingers.

4 Place plants in hole, setting rootball on the small cone of soil. Check that base of plant is level with the surrounding soil.

5 Fill in the hole and firm soil around the plant. Water thoroughly to settle the roots and soak the soil around the plant.

Tip

To keep Dusty Millers low and bushy, pinch back the tips by an inch or two several times during the growing season.

Secrets of Success

BUYING HINTS

- **Buy young, fresh-looking** Dusty Miller plants with dense foliage in six-packs or 4 in. containers.
- **Avoid buying leggy** Dusty Miller plants and any that have roots protruding from the drainage holes of their containers.

SUN & SOIL

- **Full sun.** Dusty Millers need full sun all day. In shade, the leaves lose their silvery glow and the plants become spindly.
- **Well-drained soil.** If soil is heavy clay, work in at least 1 in. of coarse sand or compost before planting.

SPECIAL ADVICE

- **The yellow blooms** of Dusty Miller tend to spoil its neat, silvery look. Pick buds as soon as they appear to discourage flowering.
- **Plant Dusty Millers** around vegetables that deer love. Its fuzzy leaves are a natural deterrent.

 Seasonal Tips

EARLY SPRING
Planting
Six weeks before last frost date, sow seeds indoors. Press seeds into soil, but do not cover. When Dusty Miller seedlings emerge, keep at about 75 degrees F. in a brightly lit location. Plant out store-bought or sown seedlings as soon as soil is warm and the plants have true leaves.

EARLY SUMMER
Taking cuttings
Propagate Dusty Miller by taking tip cuttings *(right)*.

Insert cuttings in damp sand and place in a shady location. When new growth appears, transplant to a sunny, well-drained site.

LATE SUMMER
Removing flowers
Pick buds as soon as they appear to discourage Dusty Miller from blooming.

 Plant Doctor

Dusty Millers occasionally succumb to root and stem rots, caused by various fungi that thrive in heavy, clay soils. Leaves become yellow, wilt, and die. Remove badly infected plants. To prevent disease, plant in well-drained soil and do not overwater.

Dutch Irises

Carefree jewels of the late-spring garden

Season	Special Features	Best Conditions	
Flowers in late spring or early summer	Easy to grow Good for cutting Disease resistant	Zones 5-9 Full sun Well-drained soil	 Height: 18-24 in. ◄— Spread: 4-6 in.

Bright, Graceful Blooms

Dutch Irises dance in the wind above grassy leaves, bringing color and motion to your garden.

COLORS & VARIETIES

The elegant, 4 in. blooms of Dutch Irises, so familiar from florists' bouquets, come in all shades and combinations of blue, violet, yellow, bronze, and white—all with a golden stripe on the lower petals. The colorful flowers are set high above strap-like leaves.

'Ideal' is a clear, strong blue, a color that is rare in large, showy flowers and is desirable in any garden setting. 'Blue Ribbon' is darker, verging on navy, and creates a striking accent.

Regal 'Yellow Queen'

A striking border plant

Subtle and understated, lovely 'Bronze Perfection' has bronze-edged, lilac upper petals, which are set off by bronze-streaked, yellow lower petals.

All-white 'Casablanca', with a central splash of gold, creates a cool, fresh effect with the white-and-lemon petals of 'Angel Wings'.

For purple blooms, choose from dark violet 'Purple Sensation', bright purple 'National Velvet', or lavender 'Frans Hals', with lilac-and-gold lower petals.

WHERE TO PLANT

Any flower bed or border will be all the better for a planting of these brilliant Irises. Refined enough for the most formal setting, they are also graceful and charming in odd corners of the garden.

By a stone wall or in a large rock garden, Dutch Irises will look like a colony of wildflowers and will enjoy perfect drainage. However, you may find them too tall for a small rock garden.

In a perennial bed or border, Dutch Irises, which bloom before Bearded Irises, extend the Iris season, while the grassy leaves are easily hidden after blooming ends.

In an out-of-the-way spot, plant some Dutch Irises in an informal cutting garden to cut for bouquets. The Iris bulbs are very inexpensive and the blooms last a long time in water.

'Purple Sensation' with Bounc

PERFECT PARTNERS

Dutch Irises have a light, airy look in the garden and are set off well by a backdrop of more substantial perennials or flowering shrubs.

In front of the early-blooming, rose-red 'Madame Calot' Peony, plant light blue 'Hildegarde' Irises. Bloom times will overlap, and the flower combination will keep the area colorful for a month or even more.

Highlight an early yellow Rose, such as classic 'Harrison's Yellow', with a patch of coordinating Dutch Irises—'Lemon Queen' or white-and-gold 'Marquette'.

A Fern-like clump of pale blue Jacob's Ladders wil complement blue-violet 'Blue Magic' Irises and will later

Bet and Azaleas

camouflage the dying Iris leaves in summer.

Plant classic blue 'Wedgewood' Irises among drifts of red Single Late Tulips and early yellow Dwarf Bearded Irises for a late-spring splash of color.

Delicate 'White Wedgewood'

PLANTING & AFTERCARE

YOU WILL NEED: ❏ Dutch Iris bulbs ❏ Trowel ❏ Sand ❏ Bulb fertilizer ❏ Mulch ❏ Rake

1 Plant Dutch Irises in fall, while the soil is still warm. Dig a hole 8 in. deep and 12 in. by 18 in. wide to accommodate a dozen bulbs.

2 Mix 2 in. of sand and a tablespoon of bulb fertilizer into the bottom of hole. Level soil and set bulbs 6 in. apart, pointed ends up.

3 Cover bulbs with 6 in. of soil, firm lightly, and water well. Add an inch of mulch to the area to retain moisture and keep soil warm.

4 In zones 5-7, add an additional 3-4 in. of mulch once ground has frozen. Leave in place until danger of frost has passed.

5 Rake off winter mulch in mid-spring. Deadhead faded flowers to prevent seed production. Allow foliage to die back naturally.

Tip

If summer rainfall is high, Dutch Irises will not be long-lived. Buy bulbs annually or dig up once leaves die and store.

Secrets of Success

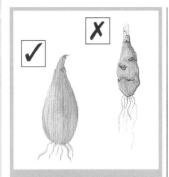

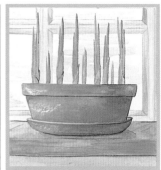

BUYING HINTS

- **Buy firm Dutch Iris** bulbs with glossy, golden tan skins. Look for bulbs with no signs of new growth from the tops.
- **Avoid soft bulbs,** those with damaged skins, and any that show green or blue mold on or under the skin.

SUN & SOIL

- **Full sun.** Dutch Irises require full sun in early summer to ripen foliage. Avoid planting in shade.
- **Well-drained soil.** Clay or sandy soils are fine as long as drainage is good. Too much moisture will prevent future blooms.

SPECIAL ADVICE

- **Pot five bulbs** in a pot for late winter flowers inside. Place in a frost-free spot and bring to a sunny window when the shoots reach 3 in. tall.
- **In clay soils,** plant Dutch Iris bulbs more shallowly than recommended.

 Seasonal Tips

 Plant Doctor

EARLY FALL
Planting
Plant Dutch Iris bulbs and mulch lightly. Pot up bulbs for forcing in winter.

LATE FALL
Mulching & Storing
In zones 5-7, apply winter mulch. Store potted bulbs in a frost-free place.

SPRING
Maintaining
Remove mulch when danger of hard frost has passed. Deadhead faded flowers, leaving foliage to die.

SUMMER
Lifting
In wet summer climates, lift, dry, and clean bulbs when foliage has withered *(below)*. Store in a cool, dark, dry place. Replant in early fall.

Penicillium, a blue or green mold, causes Dutch Iris bulbs to rot. Prevent it by storing bulbs in a dry place and allowing for plenty of air circulation between bulbs. Never buy or plant bulbs that show mold on or under the skins.

Forget-me-nots

Quick-growing, flowering mounds of blue or pink

Season	Special Features	Best Conditions	
Perennial or annual	Fragrant	Zones 3-8	
Flowers mid- to late spring	Easy care	Partial or full shade	Height: 8-18 in.
	Self-seeding	Rich, moist soil	Spread: 6-8 in.

Rugged, Blooming Groundcover

Forget-me-nots grow vigorously and bloom profusely with very little care.

COLORS & VARIETIES

Forget-me-nots are self-sufficient, dependable bloomers for the spring garden. Some varieties are annuals, living and blooming only one season. Others are perennial, blooming again year after year. Featuring clusters of blue, white, or pink flowers throughout summer, Forget-me-nots are shade-lovers that will tolerate full sun if given a steady supply of moisture.

'**Ultramarine**' and 'Blue Ball' are annual Forget-me-nots with soft, hairy leaves that are barely visible under the crowds of blue flowers. These grow 8-12 in. tall.

Perennial varieties are hardier, have thicker leaves, grow in low-creeping mats, and spread by underground roots. 'White Ball' is a slow-growing, bushy variety that produces lovely sprays of tiny, white flowers.

Forget-me-nots in a mixed bed

WHERE TO PLANT

These versatile plants are great for planting near ponds, in rock gardens, or at the front edge of a shady border.

Rock gardens in areas with cool summers are ideal sites for Forget-me-nots. The quick-spreading annual varieties will fill in between cracks and crevices, and grow around stones.

Forget-me-nots dazzle in a co

Planted in drifts around a small, garden pond, this moisture-lover will provide a symphony in blue and green.

Along a tree-lined path, Forget-me-nots provide concentrated patches of color. Plant them under a tree with wildflowers to create a naturalistic design.

PERFECT PARTNERS

The best companions for Forget-me-nots are spring-blooming bulbs and shade-tolerant plants that enjoy the same moist soil.

The upright forms of Hyacinths, Daffodils, and Tulips will sing with the

The dainty, lavender-blue blooms of 'Early Bird Blue'

ful bed with Ranunculus

profuse, lavender-blue flower clusters of 'Blue Bird'.

In a shady garden spot, combine Hostas, Maidenhair Ferns, and 'Carmine King'. The lush, summer foliage of these plants will hide the fading Forget-me-not blooms.

In a woodland bed with Scilla

PLANTING & AFTERCARE

YOU WILL NEED: ❏ 8-11 Forget-me-not plants ❏ Compost ❏ Mulch ❏ Trowel ❏ Pruning shears

1 Spread compost on top of soil in planting area. Work this into the top 4 in. of soil and water well. Dig hole for Forget-me-not.

2 Place plant in hole at same level it sat in its container. Plant seven to nine seedlings around the first, spacing all 6-8 in. apart.

3 Keep soil moist by watering at ground level regularly or by using a soaker hose. Remove grass or weeds by hand.

4 Mulch around perennial forms in late fall. Annual forms will self-seed, so shake the spent flower blossoms where you want more plants.

5 Prune back the spent blossoms and overly long stems soon after blooming to control the growth of Forget-me-not plants.

Tip

Remove faded blooms and lay them at the base of your Forget-me-nots. This will help annual and biennial types reseed and grow plants next year.

Secrets of Success

BUYING HINTS

- **Buy young, green** plants in 4 in. pots with signs of buds already showing.
- **Avoid Forget-me-nots** that have a white, powdery coating on their foliage. Do not buy plants without buds or you may have to wait two years for blooms.

SUN & SOIL

- **Partial shade.** Forget-me-nots need to be shaded from sun in warm climates.
- **Moist, well-drained** soil. Forget-me-nots can survive in dry, summer soil if they are kept moist in the spring. Add some compost to retain moisture in the soil.

SPECIAL ADVICE

- **Forget-me-nots** can be incredible, long-lasting cut flowers if you cut stems when flowers are just buds.
- **Perennial varieties** will quickly spread to fill in new areas with many plants if you move one or two from an established flower bed.

 Seasonal Tips

FALL
Preparing
Prepare the soil for Forget-me-nots by adding compost or well-rotted manure.

EARLY SPRING
Buying
Purchase Forget-me-nots in bloom and plant.

SPRING
Cutting
Trim back spent Forget-me-nots. You can compost the cut blooms or return them to the garden (right) as food for next year's seedlings.

SUMMER
Watering
Keep Forget-me-not plants moist during hot weather, using a soaker hose or overhead watering to protect next year's young plants.

 Plant Doctor

Forget-me-nots are very susceptible to mildew if grown in dry soil. Look for a powdery, white film on leaves. Uproot any infected plants and throw them out. Add organic matter to soil and water more regularly to prevent this disease.

Foxgloves

Towering spikes of colorful, cup-shaped blooms

Season	*Special Features*	*Best Conditions*	
Biennial	Self-seeder	Zones 4-8	
Blooms in summer	Poisonous	Full sun	Height: 3-8 ft.
	Excellent cut flower	Moist, well-drained soil	Spread: 2-3 ft.

Bell-shaped Blooms

Foxgloves are the skyscrapers of the garden, adding colorful vertical lines to summer designs.

COLORS & VARIETIES

Foxgloves are tall, stately plants that carry purple, yellow, rose, or white, bell-shaped blooms on long spikes with darker, interior splotches or freckles. The flower stalks grow from a large rosette of leaves.

Foxglove reseeds easily and a single purple plant is capable of producing multicolored offspring. Most Foxgloves bloom biennially, growing foliage the first year and blooming and dying the second, although some perennial forms are available.

Yellow Foxglove *(Digitalis grandiflora)* grows just 3 ft. tall with creamy yellow flowers that are flecked with brown.

Rusty Foxglove *(D. ferruginea)* features pale orange-brown blooms on 4 ft. long stalks, while English Foxglove forms ivory white, purple, shell pink, or deep rose flowers dotted with brown or scarlet.

WHERE TO PLANT

Its sturdy, upright, flower-lined spikes make Foxglove a distinctive plant to use as a backdrop for other flowers, among flowering shrubs, or as elegant specimen plants in the summer garden.

In flower borders, plant Foxgloves in the back of the bed with Shasta Daisies or Peonies in the foreground. Perennials that have round flower heads provide a stunning contrast to Foxglove's vertical lines.

Among flowering shrubs, Foxglove is tall enough to emerge from the crowd, and tough enough to compete with larger plants for food and water.

In naturalistic settings, Foxglove is right at home, able to thrive at the base of old stumps and rotting logs. Planted with Ferns along a woodland walk, Foxglove will reseed and bloom in colorful colonies for years.

Foxgloves in a cut-flower gar

PERFECT PARTNERS

The best companions for Foxglove are flowers and plants that complement its tall, narrow form and dramatic blooms.

Combine classic cut flowers, such as Sweet William, Snapdragons, and Roses, with the strawberry pink Merton Foxglove.

Summer-blooming annuals, such as Petunias, Geraniums, and Alyssum, thrive in the same soil and share the same bloom time as Foxgloves. Combine bright annuals to vibrate against the white blooms of the Foxglove 'Alba'.

Spring bulbs provide bursts of color when the ric

'Alba' offers scarlet accents

Pink Foxgloves and Roses

n with Peonies and Daisies

pink, rose, purple, and white shades of the 'Excelsior Hybrids' are not in bloom. The round clump of the Foxglove's foliage will screen the bulbs' foliage as they yellow and fade.

Foxgloves in a summer bed

PLANTING & AFTERCARE

YOU WILL NEED: ❑ Foxglove plant ❑ Compost ❑ Mulch ❑ Trowel ❑ Wire hanger

1 Dig a hole wide enough for the width of the Foxglove plant. Add a heaping trowelful of compost to the hole and mix it into the soil.

2 Set the plant in the hole at the same level it was growing at before. Add soil and firm gently around the roots. Water well.

3 Lay a 1 in. layer of pine bark around the newly planted Foxglove. Fertilize in early spring before the plant sends up a flower spike.

4 Stake tall plants. Untwist a wire hanger, looping the hooked handle around the stem and sticking the other end into ground.

5 Lay spent flowers on a bed of soil so that ripening seeds can fall easily, or break off a capsule of dried seeds and scatter them.

Tip

When flowers fade, cut the main spike where it emerges from foliage. New spikes will sprout as side shoots.

Secrets of Success

BUYING HINTS

- **Buy large Foxglove** plants with many leaves. Buy one-year-old plants to ensure they will bloom the year you buy them.
- **Avoid pots** filled with many young seedlings, as they will need two seasons before blooming.

SUN & SOIL

- **Full sun.** Foxgloves are very adaptable plants, but will grow straightest if they receive direct sunlight.
- **Well-drained, rich soil.** Soil enriched with compost will produce the best blooms, but Foxgloves will grow even in poor soils.

SPECIAL ADVICE

- **Foxgloves are said to** have a growth-stimulating effect on many nearby plants, particularly Pines.
- **Keep all children** away from Foxglove plants, as the blooms, foliage, and seeds are all extremely poisonous if eaten.

 ## Seasonal Tips

SPRING
Buying
Purchase Foxglove plants and set them in the garden while the weather is still cool.

SUMMER
Staking
Support tall Foxgloves as necessary if they start to show signs of leaning. Protect them from wind if you are expecting a summer storm.

LATE SUMMER
Reseeding
Lay the spent flower stalks on the ground where you want

plants to grow, or sprinkle the seeds while they are still in their dried capsules.

WINTER
Mulching
Lightly mulch around roots of young seedlings *(below)*.

 ## Plant Doctor

Distorted leaves, stems, and buds are signs of Foxglove aphids. These tiny, brown or white insects suck out Foxglove's sap. Wash them from plants with a strong stream of water. If they persist, control with insecticidal soap spray.

Hostas

Gorgeous foliage and flowers for shady corners

Season	*Special Features*	*Best Conditions*	
Perennial	✓ Easy care	🌐 Zones 3-9	
❋ Flowers in mid-summer	🕷 Disease resistant	☀ Full to partial shade	Height: 18-48 in.
		🔨 Moist, rich soil	◀ Spread: 12-48 in.

Classic Shade Lover

Fill troublesome damp, dark garden areas with the glossy, elegant foliage of Hostas.

COLORS & VARIETIES

Hostas, also known as Plantain Lilies, are ideal for providing colorful and textural interest in damp, dark corners. This wide-spreading plant is available in many different shades of green and blue, as well as variegated varieties with white, silver, or gold patches or stripes on the leaves.

'Frances Williams' is a large Hosta that will spread to 4 ft. Its medium green leaves are trimmed in gold. Like many Hostas, the leaves are deeply patterned with a seersucker design. 'Krossa Regal' features sophisticated, vase-shaped leaves of blue-gray that grow to 24 in. high.

Most Hostas send up long stems carrying bell-shaped flowers in mid-summer. The blooms range from the light purple flowers of *Hosta fortunei albopicata* to the elegant, bright white blooms of 'Grandiflora'.

'Nigressen elatior' Hosta

WHERE TO PLANT

Hostas are tough plants that grow well in many areas, but are truly at home in shade.

Ring the base of a tree with a necklace of Hostas. Use variegated varieties to add some brightness to the filtered shade. Try 'Ginko Craig' for its silver-edged, sword-shaped leaves.

In the dense shade cast along the side of a house, plant Hostas as a lush, low

Pink Astilbe with H. montana,

border. Try 'Albomarginata's' oval-shaped leaves edged with pure white margins.

In the shadow of thick hedges, Hostas provide a tropical setting. The bright green 'Royal Standard' makes a magnificent mound of color in large plantings.

PERFECT PARTNERS

Hostas are best paired with other shade-loving plants, and their gentle curves and soft shades go well with a range of flowers and plants.

Contrast the smooth texture of Hosta leaves with the lacy foliage of Ferns. Plant Ostrich Feather Ferns behind the 2 ft. mounds of *H. sieboldiana elegans*.

Hostas bordering a planting of Asiatic Lilies

plantaginea, and 'Honey Bells'

Hostas are often paired with another shade-loving perennial, Astilbe. Mix *H. minor alba* for stunning, white flowers with the shorter, white blooms of the Astilbe 'Bridal Veil.'

Hostas in a woodland design

PLANTING & AFTERCARE

YOU WILL NEED: ❏ Hosta plants ❏ Trowel ❏ Peat moss ❏ Shredded pine bark ❏ Pruning shears

1 Dig hole twice as large as pot, after the danger of frost has passed. Fill hole with a mix of soil and two shovelfuls of peat moss.

2 Remove the Hosta from its container, being careful not to damage the roots. Leave the rootball as intact as possible.

3 Place the plant in the hole. The base of the Hosta should be level with the ground. Fill in around the Hosta with soil. Firm well.

4 Water thoroughly to completely soak the soil around the plant. Apply shredded pine bark around the Hosta as a mulch.

5 After blooms fade, cut the flower stalks back. Remove slug-damaged leaves and replenish mulch as needed during the season.

Dollar Sense

Grow Hostas for free by dividing. After two or three years, dig up in early spring. Use a knife to cut crowns, keeping three to five buds on each piece, and replant.

Secrets of Success

BUYING HINTS

- **Buy dense plants** in pots. Look for those with several leaf buds and at least one unfolded leaf to verify foliage color and texture.
- **Avoid wilted,** container-grown plants in dry soil. Hostas become stressed in pots allowed to go dry.

SUN & SOIL

- **Full to partial shade.** Most Hostas keep their color better in shade. Variegated varieties can tolerate full sun if you water frequently.
- **Rich, moist soil.** Add plenty of organic matter, such as compost, to increase nutrients and soil drainage.

SPECIAL ADVICE

- **An economical way to** grow Hostas is to start bareroot plants in pots on a windowsill in early spring.
- **Plant early spring-**blooming bulbs around your Hostas. The bulbs' dying foliage will be hidden by the new foliage of the Hostas.

 Seasonal Tips

 *Plant Doctor*

EARLY SPRING
Dividing
Divide older, established Hostas when soil is warm enough to easily be worked. Dig down with a shovel and separate the main clump of the plant, divide in half, and then replant each.

LATE SPRING
Planting
When all danger of frost has passed, plant potted Hostas in a shady bed or border. Add plenty of organic matter to the soil as you prepare the planting area.

FALL
Mulching
Where winter temperatures fall near zero, mulch around the Hostas *(below)* to provide winter protection as foliage begins to turn yellow.

Slugs are the standard enemies of Hostas. Large holes in the leaves are signs of slugs. To prevent these pests, spread diatomaceous earth, available at garden centers, around the plants; or place a saucer of beer next to your Hostas.

Impatiens

Beautiful and versatile bedding plants

Season	Special Features	Best Conditions	
A Annual	✓ **Very easy care**	**All zones**	
✽ **Flowers early summer to first frost**	**Very resistant to disease**	**Full sun to full shade**	
		Well-drained soil	Height: 4-28 in. ◄—Spread: 8-24 in.─

Stunning in Sun or Shade

The amazing number of varieties allows you to create your own favorite color scheme.

COLORS & VARIETIES

Double-flowered Impatiens look like small Roses. Single-flowered varieties are best for mass plantings. Choose 'Eclipse' for orange blooms and pointed leaves; 'Accent Stars' for stripes or splashes of color on its leaves; 'Wink and Blink' for fluorescent colors and distinctive marks; or a larger New Guinea hybrid with striped leaves.

WHERE TO PLANT

Impatiens are amazingly versatile. You can plant them in a bed or border, in any

Transform a dull facade with a vibrant mix of Impatiens walle

New Guinea Impatiens

Impatiens 'Elfin White'

kind of container, and even in the deep shade of trees. No matter where you plant them, Impatiens are sure to dazzle with vibrant color.

Under a tree, plant the 'Tempo Series' hybrids in calm pastel shades and 'Super Elfin' hybrids in vivid neon colors. Both provide strong highlights in the deep shade cast by a tree. Water well, as tree roots may steal moisture from the little plants.

In hanging baskets, Impatiens are ideal since they flower over a long period. Double-flowered 'Extra Dwarf' hybrids mature quickly and spread widely.

In a terra-cotta pot, grow 'Blackberry Ice' for white flowers splashed with purple.

Impatiens planted with Salvia

PERFECT PARTNERS

Fuse multicolored Impatiens with single-colored flowers or single-colored Impatiens with variegated foliage.

'Red Star', which bears scarlet flowers with white, star-shaped markings, will shine when surrounded by a sea of white Alyssum.

ıa and Petunias

A pot of variegated Impatiens

Create an old-fashioned look by choosing red or pink 'Confection' Impatiens to complement the variegated foliage of Wax Begonias.

Impatiens come alive against the deep burgundy foliage of Coleus. Allow the rose red blooms of 'Lipstick' to vibrate against this foliage plant's scintillating hues.

PLANTING & AFTERCARE

YOU WILL NEED: ❑ Impatiens seedlings ❑ Garden fork ❑ Garden compost or fertilizer ❑ Mulch

1 After the last frost, dig a hole large enough to accommodate the rootball of the seedling. Loosen soil and dig in some garden compost.

2 Push the seedling out of its plastic cell. Loosen the rootball so that it can grow more easily, but do not lose too much soil.

3 Plant the seedling to the same level it sat in the flat. Replace the soil all around the plant without disturbing its roots.

4 Pat the soil down, making sure stem and roots are held firmly. Water thoroughly, and place mulch around your Impatiens.

Dollar Sense

Grow Impatiens the following year from cuttings. The New Guinea hybrids are best suited for this. Cut off healthy shoots in early fall. Dip them in hormone rooting powder, then plant them in a tray of growing medium, such as perlite. You should be able to plant the new seedlings the following spring.

Secrets of Success

BUYING HINTS

- **Buy small seedlings** in a tray. Choose compact seedlings with deep green leaves. If at least one seedling is in bloom, you can verify the color.
- **Avoid leggy plants** with yellowing leaves and those that are fully in flower, as they may be potbound.

SUN & SOIL

- **Sun or shade.** Impatiens are one of the few annual bedding plants that are able to tolerate even full shade under a tree. Be sure to keep them well watered.
- **Well-drained soil.** To keep your plants healthy, add some compost or all-purpose fertilizer to soil.

SPECIAL ADVICE

- **For fuller growth,** cut off the top third of your seedlings with a pair of scissors immediately after you plant them.
- **Deadheading is not** necessary, as Impatiens are "self-cleaners"—old blooms are continuously replaced by new ones until first frost.

 ## Seasonal Tips

 ## Plant Doctor

EARLY SPRING
Sowing
The seeds are tiny and difficult to handle. Sow in a seed tray *(right)*, and thin out plants as they grow.

LATE SPRING
Planting
Plant seedlings you have bought or grown after the soil has warmed in late spring. Plant in early morning or evening. Avoid planting midday because excess heat may stress the plants. Harden off seedlings you have grown for a day before planting.

EARLY FALL
Lifting
Impatiens will flower up until the first frost. Pull up and discard them, or add them to your compost heap.

Impatiens are easy-care plants, resistant to most diseases and unappealing to animals and insects. They are, however, seriously affected by lack of water. If you are too busy to water them, consider utilizing a drip-watering system.

Marigolds
Abundant blooms for sunny spots

Season	Special Features	Best Conditions	
Annual	✓ **Very easy care**	🌐 **All zones**	
Flowers from spring until frost	❋ **Disease and insect resistant**	☼ **Full sun**	
	✂ **Good for cutting**	⬟ **Moist, acidic soil**	

Petunias, and Begonias

Marigolds with red Salvia

PLANTING & AFTERCARE

YOU WILL NEED: ❏ Marigold seedlings ❏ Garden trowel ❏ Peat moss or compost ❏ Weed-free straw

1 After the last frost, prepare the bed for the Marigolds by loosening the soil at least 8 in. deep. Add peat moss or compost to clay soils.

2 Dig a hole the size of the seedling's rootball. Remove the seedling from the cell, disturbing the roots as little as possible.

3 Plant the Marigold seedling in the hole and pat the soil around it. Repeat this process until all of your seedlings are planted.

4 Water well with gentle spray. Apply enough water to seep down past the rootball. Spread mulch, such as weed-free straw, around seedlings.

5 Remove faded flowers by carefully pinching them off between your thumb and forefinger. This will encourage new Marigold blooms.

Dollar Sense

Dry Marigold flowers for their seeds. Crumble the blooms and collect the seeds, storing them in a paper envelope.

Bright Spots of Gold

Marigolds add splashes of sunshine-colored brilliance to any garden bed or border.

COLORS & VARIETIES

There are two basic types of this rugged flowering plant: African and French. The Africans feature smaller, ball-shaped flower heads, while French varieties grow much bigger with Daisy-like flowers. Each type offers a wide range of colors, from yellow to deep orange.

Choose dwarf varieties as edging for beds. 'Janie Tangerine' has bright orange flowers and grows 8-10 in. high. Alternate these with 'Janie Primrose', a soft yellow Marigold, for an orange-and-yellow checkerboard.

For a more delicate look, plant 'España Granada', a bright gold variety with rusty red drops radiating from the flower's center.

WHERE TO PLANT

Marigolds thrive almost anywhere as long as they receive a generous amount of sunlight and a continuous

Marigolds edging Zinnias

The French 'Queen Sophia'

The African 'Cracker Jack'

supply of water. They are equally at home in the ground or in containers.

Brighten narrow, sunny borders with multicolored dwarf varieties, such as 'Little Devil Fire' in reddish gold, or 'Queen Sophia' with its bushy gold blooms. You can plant tall varieties, such as 'Gold Giant', throughout the middle to fill out this golden-hued sunny planting.

Add depth to a mixed flower bed by planting different sizes of Marigolds throughout the bed, with Petunias, Begonias, and other flowering annuals.

Create fun container gardens with a mix of tall, medium, and dwarf varieties in different-sized pots.

A mixed border of Marigolds,

PERFECT PARTNERS

The various shades of yellow and gold complement a host of vibrant flowers.

Accent your Marigolds with delicate, low-growing border annuals, such as Alyssum. For a striking duo, combine purple Alyssum with the large, deep orange blooms of 'Toreador'.

The fiery sunset hues of Gloriosa Daisies, Zinnias, and Strawflowers, provide dazzling backdrops for shorter Marigolds in similar shades. Match the gold, mahogany, or orange blooms of the 8 in. tall 'Boy-o-boy' with the rust, gold, and deep tangerine blooms of the 'Zenith Hybrids' Zinnias.

Secrets of Success

BUYING HINTS

- **Buy seedlings** in four- or six-cell flats. Look for very bushy, compact plants with lush, deep green growth.
- **Avoid limp**, leggy plants with withered leaves. Young plants that have been poorly cared for will produce a limited number of blooms.

SUN & SOIL

- **Full sun.** These bright annuals thrive in direct sun. Given proper sun, most varieties will continue to flower all summer.
- **Well-drained soil.** Marigolds can tolerate most soils, but they bloom less in poorly drained soils.

SPECIAL ADVICE

- **Plant your Marigolds** in masses of single colors for a more dramatic effect. If you use both yellow and orange blooms, consider broad stripes of single colors.
- **Use only low-nitrogen** fertilizer. Excess nitrogen causes less blooms.

Seasonal Tips

EARLY SPRING
Sowing
Marigolds are easy annuals to grow from seed. Sow the seeds in growing trays or individual peat pots and place by a sunny window until the soil outside warms.

LATE SPRING
Planting
After the last frost, plant seedlings in the garden. Put them outdoors during the day and bring them in at night for a week to harden them off before planting outside. Cover with a layer of mulch.

SUMMER
Deadheading & Feeding
Remove faded blooms. Spray with a low-nitrogen liquid fertilizer every two weeks. Water at least once a day during dry spells or in extremely hot weather.

FALL
Protecting
Marigolds will flower well into fall if you provide just a little protection against the elements. Cover Marigolds with clear plastic row covers, available at garden centers, to enjoy blooms in autumn.

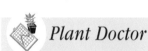

Plant Doctor

Marigolds resist most diseases and pests. Most plant damage results from using a hose with a strong stream of water. Use drip irrigation whenever possible. A soaker hose is a good choice for a border or narrow planting strips.

Nicotianas

Versatile annuals for fragrance and form

Season	Special Features	Best Conditions	
Annual	Easy to grow	All zones	
❋ Flowers from summer to frost	Good for cutting	Full sun to partial shade	Height: 1-5 ft.
	Poisonous	Rich, well-drained soil	◄ Spread: 12-18 in.

Sweet, Floral Trumpets

Fill the evening air with the delicate, perfumed fragrance from fluttering sprays of Nicotiana.

COLORS & VARIETIES

Airy Nicotianas, also called Flowering Tobacco, bloom in pinks, reds, yellows, white, and even pale green. The soft, slightly sticky leaves of the plant form low rosettes beneath taller flower stalks.

One foot 'Domino' and 'Metro' dwarfs tolerate heat more readily than other varieties and bloom in the full range of colors. 'Domino Salmon Pink' prefers dappled shade in warm summer areas, as does 'Metro Mixed'.

The 15-18 in. 'Nicki' strain blooms in every color from late spring to frost and holds up well under harsh weather conditions. 'Nicki Bright Pink' is popular for its prolific pink blooms.

The 2-4 ft. 'Sensation Mixed' blooms in every Nicotiana color and is a favorite for its intense evening fragrance. Taller still, lightly fragrant *Nicotiana sylvestris* produces pendant clusters of 3 in., white flowers that open fully in

Nicotiana 'Lime Green'

Brilliant 'Nicki Red' in a bed

evenings, in partial shade, and also on cloudy or overcast days.

WHERE TO PLANT

Plant Nicotianas in beds with other summer-blooming annuals and perennials, in borders with shrubs, in containers on patios and decks, or in cottage and cutting gardens.

Delight your senses on a small patio surrounded by a bed devoted to one of the taller varieties, such as the white 'Grandiflora'. The sweetly scented, lavish flowers appear on 3 ft. stems.

Decorate a partly shaded entry with sweetly scented 'Breakthrough Mixed' and taller 'Sensation White'. Their soft fragrance will welcome evening visitors.

Alternate varieties lacking fragrance, such as the rich red, 18-20 in. 'Crimson Bedder', in a bed or border with fragrant annuals and perennials for a bed full of daylight scents.

'Shade Star' contrasts in color

PERFECT PARTNERS

Like other popular annuals, Nicotianas work well planted closely for a simple, but striking, summer-long display that blends easily with more permanent plantings.

Plant bushy, 24 in., red 'Crimson Rock' in colorful beds among Penstemons 'Garnet', Dahlias, and Yarrows. Edge the bed with Bethlehem Sages mixed with the lovely pink-and-white flowers of 'Appleblossom'.

Between shrubs, fill spaces left by Tulips and Daffodils with the 2 ft. tall, yellow-green 'Lime Green'. Balance a large Viburnum or Dogwood with bushy, 2-3 ft. 'Sutton's Scarlet'.

nd form with Shirley Poppies

Introduce height to a large container with 4 ft. tall 'Peace Pipe' and its dramatic, 3 in., tubular, white flowers. For a smaller container, accent draping, silver-leaved Helichrysum with rose-red 'Rubella' and low mounds of 'Hot Tip' Begonias.

Hot pink 'Domino'

PLANTING & AFTERCARE

YOU WILL NEED: ❏ Nicotiana seeds ❏ Peat pots ❏ Mist sprayer ❏ Plastic wrap ❏ Heating mats ❏ Shears

1 **Six weeks before** last frost date, moisten peat pots in a water-filled tray until they are saturated. Pour off any remaining water.

2 **Sow three seeds** in each pot. Settle soil with a spray of water. Cover with clear plastic wrap, which lets light through.

3 **Keep the pots** evenly moist by misting periodically. Keep warm (70-75 degrees F.) with heating mats beneath tray.

4 **Snip off all** but the strongest seedling in each pot. Pinch back to encourage side branching. Gradually expose outdoors.

5 **To transplant,** slit pot sides, set 8-12 in. apart, and cover peat completely with soil. Keep moist and apply fertilizer monthly.

Troubleshooter

If young plant leaves begin to yellow, it may be from a lack of nutrients, or too much water. Keep plants moist, not wet, and fertilize every two weeks.

Secrets of Success

BUYING HINTS

SUN & SOIL

SPECIAL ADVICE

- **Buy seeds** from nursery catalogs or garden centers in winter. In late spring, purchase plants in six-packs labeled for color and height.
- **Avoid plants** with dark or yellow spots on their leaves, which may indicate a fungal or viral infection.

- **Full sun** to partial shade. Hybrids do best in full sun with ample moisture. Especially fragrant varieties do best in partial shade.
- **Fertile, well-drained,** moist soil. Before planting, amend soil with compost and add granular fertilizer.

- **White-flowering** varieties are most fragrant late in the day. Plant where you can enjoy their scent.
- **Smokers often carry** tobacco mosaic virus, picked up from cigarettes, and should wash their hands before handling plants.

 ## Seasonal Tips

SPRING
Planting
After last frost, set out seedlings and plants from nurseries. Mulch roots to conserve soil moisture.

SUMMER
Maintaining
Irrigate as needed to keep soil evenly moist. Fertilize monthly to promote continued blooms. Stake taller forms if they become unstable in wind or rain. Cut flower stalks before seeds set to reduce self-sowing and to promote reblooming.

FALL
Composting
After the Nicotianas have finished flowering, cut them to the ground with hand pruners, or mow entire beds of Nicotianas (below). Chop up plants and add them to your compost pile.

 ## Plant Doctor

Huge, light green hornworm caterpillars will feed on the stems and leaves of Nicotianas, leaving the plant looking chewed. Although unsightly and sometimes voracious, these worms are not dangerous to humans. Pick them off by hand and destroy them.

Best Beds and Borders

The works of a person that builds begin immediately to decay; while those of him who plants begin directly to improve. In this, planting promises a more lasting pleasure than building.
— *William Shenstone*

WEEDS PRODUCE abundant seeds that can remain dormant in the soil for a very long time, germinating when brought to the soil's surface. Weeding early in the season pays great dividends, so remove these destructive plants before they can produce flowers and seeds.

CASH IN ON FALL perennial plant sales, but have a plan for where you will put the new purchases. If permanent locations can't be decided upon, put plants in a nursery bed, with markers indicating their species.

SLUGS ARE A PERENNIAL PROBLEM for Coleus and Hostas. To deter slugs, spread a barrier of diatomaceous earth or wood ash around individual plants. Alternatively, plastic margarine tubs filled with stale beer make effective slug traps. All of these methods need replenishment after rains.

TO INCREASE THE SIZE and number of blooms in your beds and borders, avoid using fertilizers that have more nitrogen than phosphorus or potassium in them. This is important because nitrogen tends to stimulate foliage and stem growth at the expense of flowers and roots.

TO AVOID PLANTING TINY SEEDS such as those of Nicotiana and Salvia too densely, mix them with a teaspoon of dry sand. Sprinkle the mixture on the surface of soil, and then spray water from a mister to keep seeds moist.

Nature's Way

The best time to control Japanese beetles is not when the adults are present during summer, but during fall and spring when their grubs are alive in the soil. Apply beneficial nematodes to the surface of lawns and garden soil in spring after the soil temperature rises above 55 degrees F. Beneficial nematodes can be purchased at most nurseries and garden centers.

December
- ❏ Prune fall-blooming shrubs.
- ❏ Evaluate garden successes and failures of the year and start planning for next year.

January
- ❏ Read through gardening catalogs and order seeds.

February
- ❏ Start seeds of species such as Coleus that have a long maturation time.

March
- ❏ Carefully remove winter mulch if weather has warmed.
- ❏ Divide perennials and transplant to new locations.
- ❏ Add soil amendments such as bone meal or compost.

April
- ❏ Dig beds.
- ❏ Weed established beds and borders, and install or repair edging.
- ❏ Rejuvenate compost pile.
- ❏ Many annual seeds can be planted outdoors now.
- ❏ Purchase and plant species that grow best in cool weather.

May
- ❏ Transplant seedlings in regions where danger of frost has passed.
- ❏ Pull young weeds as they emerge.
- ❏ Make cuttings of Artemisia.
- ❏ Plant seeds of late summer flowers such as Cosmos.

June
- ❏ Deadhead annuals and perennials to prolong flowering season.
- ❏ Weed beds and borders.
- ❏ Replenish compost where necessary.

July
- ❏ Continue deadheading annuals and perennials.
- ❏ Fertilize late summer perennials.

August
- ❏ Continue deadheading annuals and perennials.
- ❏ Divide Irises.

September
- ❏ Plan new borders, island beds, or bed expansions for next year. Apply a thick layer of mulch to kill grass.
- ❏ Suspend deadheading.
- ❏ Dig up tender perennials for indoor use.
- ❏ Plant spring-flowering bulbs as weather cools.

October
- ❏ Mulch beds and borders.
- ❏ Transplant biennials such as Foxgloves to new locations before the ground freezes.
- ❏ Collect and store dry seeds for next year.
- ❏ Pull up late weeds and dead annuals.

November
- ❏ Prune back dead plant remains and put in compost pile.
- ❏ Bunker up compost pile in areas with cold winters.
- ❏ Dig up tender bulbs and tubers for winter storage.

A *Aconitum henryi* 38
African Marigolds 28-29
Ageratums
    garden designs 18, 24-25
    planting and care tips 63-66
Allium 14, 44
Alcea rosea (Hollyhock) 30
Annuals 34
Annual Salvias, tips for 67-70
Aphids 106
Artemisias
    garden designs 14, 20-21
    planting and care tips 71-74
Asters 38
Azalea 44

B Baby's Breath 26
Bacillus thuringiensis (Bt) 66
Balloon Flower 18
Bedding Begonias
    garden design 28-29
    planting and care tips 75-78
Beds. *See* Companion planting;
Deadheading; Diseases; Edging beds;
Garden ideas; Island beds; Mulch making;
Pests; *specific plants*; Weed control
Beetles 90
Bellflowers
    Clustered Bellflowers 38
    Great Bellflowers (*Campanula
    latifolia*) 12-13
    planting and care tips 79-82
Bidens 26
Bishop's Weed 22
Blue False Indigo 38
Blue Fescue 22
Blue Flax 14
Blue plants 18, 22
Bold flowers and leaves 14
Border of Cool-hued Perennials . . . 35-38
Borders. *See* Companion planting;
Deadheading; Diseases; Edging beds;
Garden ideas; Island beds; Mulch making;

Pests; *specific plants;* Weed control
Brick (edging) 52
Bronze Fennel 14
Buying bedding plants 102, 106

C *Campanula carpatica* 30
Campanula latifolia
    (Great Bellflowers) 12–13
Campis 34
Carpet Bugle 22
Caterpillars 66, 122
Catmint 18, 38
Cedar edging 52
China Asters 26
Chinese Forget-me-nots 30
Chrysanthemum 38
Chrysanthemum multicaule 24-25
Clary Sage 26, 32-33
Cleaning up for fall 66, 70
Clematis 34
Clustered Bellflower 38
Cockscomb 34
Colchicum byzantinum 38
Coleus
    Common Coleus 22
    garden design 32-33
    planting and care tips 83-86
Common Coleus 22
Common Valerian 36-37
Companion planting
    for Ageratums 64-65
    for Annual Salvias 69
    for Artemisias 72-73
    for Bedding Begonias 76-77
    for Bellflowers 80-81
    for Coleus 84-85
    for Cosmos 88-89
    for Dusty Millers 92-93
    for Dutch Irises 96–97
    for Forget-me-nots 100-101
    for Foxgloves 104-105
    for Hostas 108-109
    for Impatiens 112-113

for Marigolds 116-117
for Nicotianas 120-121
Composting 122
Concrete blocks (edging) 52
Coneflower 18
Contrasts of Color and Texture 11-14
Coral Bells 36-37
Corydalis solida 38
Cosmos
  garden design 16-17
  planting and care tips 87-90
Creating Bands of Color 15-18
Cuttings 86, 94

D Daffodils 38
Dahlias 18, 26
Daisies
  Gloriosa Daisies 30
  Livingstone Daisies 30
  Swan River Daisies 26
Deadheading
  how to 41-44
  in summer 66, 118
Dicentra eximia 38
Digitalis lutea 18
Disbudding 44
Diseases
  mildew 102
  mold and penicillium 98
  root rot 94
  septoria leaf spot fungus 82
  stem rot 94
  verticillium wilt 70
Dividing 74, 82, 110
Dusty Millers
  garden design 24-25
  planting and care tips 91-94
Dutch Irises, tips for 95-98

E Edging beds 49-52
Edging plants 26
English Ivy 22
Eremurus robustus 30

Erythronium 38

F Fall tips 90, 118
Farewell-to-spring 30
Fertilizing 86
Fine flowers and leaves 14
Flowers, removing 74, 94
Forest-loving Geraniums 30
Forget-me-nots
  Chinese Forget-me-nots 30
  garden design 12-13
  planting and care tips 99-102
Formosan Toad Lily 38
Fothergilla 20-21
Foxgloves
  garden design 36-37
  planting and care tips 103-106
Fragrant Olive 22

G Garden ideas. *See also* Companion
planting; Deadheading; Diseases;
Edging beds; Island beds; Mulch making;
Pests; *specific plants;* Weed control
  Border of Cool-hued Perennials . 35-38
  Contrasts of Color and Texture . . 11-14
  Creating Bands of Color 15-18
  Rainbow-colored Flower Bed . . . 27-30
  Red Summer Border 31-34
  Subtle Foliage Colors in a Border 19-22
  Tiers of Pastel Hues 23-26
Geraniums 30, 34, 44
German Statice 18
Giant Allium 14
Globe Amaranth 30
Globe Thistle 14
Gloriosa Daisies 30
Gold Dust Plant 22
Golden Oregano 14
Gold foliage 22
Gray foliage 22
Great Bellflowers (*Campanula
latifolia*) 12-13
Green foliage 22

INDEX

H Heuchera 34
Hibiscus 18, 34
Hollyhock 18
Alcea rosea 30
Hostas, tips for 107-110
Hosta sieboldiana 14
Hosta tokudama 22
Hosta ventricosa 12-13
Hyacinth 44
Hydrangea 44

I Impatiens
garden designs . . . 24-25, 28-29, 32-33
planting and care tips 111-114
Imperata 14, 34
Insects. See Pests
Irises
Dutch Irises 95-98
Tall Bearded Irises 36-37
Iris pallida 12-13
Island beds 53-56
Ivy, English 22

J Japanese beetles 90
Japanese Maple 22
Juniper 22
Jupiter's Beard 14

L Lamb's-ears 20-21, 36-37
Landscape timbers (edging) 52
Larkspur 30
Laurentia 26
Lavatera 18
Lifting 78, 98, 114
Lily 14, 38
Livingstone Daisy 30
Lobelia 26
Love-lies-bleeding 30, 34
Low plants 26, 30

M Maiden Pinks 14, 18
Maintaining . . . 56, 82, 90, 98, 122
Maltese-cross 14

Marigolds
African Marigolds 28-29
deadheading 44
garden designs 16-17, 18, 26
planting and care tips 115-118
Marvel-of-Peru 30
Mealy-cup Sage 28-29
Medium plants 26, 30
Mildew 102
Mold and penicillium 98
Mulch, making
applications 82, 98, 106, 110
how to 57-60
Musk Mallow 38

N Narcissus 44
Nicotianas
garden design 16-17, 24-25
planting and care tips 119-122

O Ornamental Rhubarb 14
Ostrich Feather Fern 20-21

P Pansy 26, 30, 36-37
Pavers (edging) 52
Penstemon 38
Peony 38
Perennials 34, 38
Periwinkle 22, 26, 28-29
Pests
aphids 106
caterpillars 66, 122
Japanese beetles 90
slugs 78, 86, 110
snails 78, 86
spider mites 74
Petunia 16-17, 26
Phlox 16-17
Pink foliage 18, 22
Polka-dot Plant 26
Pruning 74
Purple flowers 18

INDEX

R

Railroad ties (edging) 52
Rainbow-colored Flower Bed   27-30
Red foliage 18, 22
Red Summer Border 31-34
Rhododendron 44
Root rot 94
Rose-of-Sharon 20-21
Rose Periwinkle 26, 28-29
Roses 34
Rudbeckia 14, 18

S

Sage
Clary Sage 26, 32-33
  Mealy-cup Sage 28-29
  Scarlet Sage 28-29, 32-33
Salvias 18, 67-70
Salvia splendens (Scarlet Sage) 32-33
Scarlet Firethorn 34
Scarlet Sage 28-29
Scarlet Sage (Salvia splendens) 32-33
Sedum 34
Seeding 106
Septoria leaf spot fungus 82
Short plants 30
Shrubs 34
Slugs 78, 86, 110
Snails 78, 86
Snapdragon 26
Snow-in-summer 14
Soil preparation 102
Sowing 66, 70, 78, 114, 118
Spider mites 74
Staking 106
Stem rot 94
Stone (edging) 52
Subtle Foliage Colors in a Border . . 19-22
Sunflower 18
Swan River Daisy 26
Sweet Alyssum 30
Sweet William 30

T

Tall Bearded Irises 36-37
Tall plants 26, 30

Tellima grandiflora 22
Tiers of Pastel Hues 23-26
Trimming 102
Tulip 38, 44

V

Valerian, Common 36-37
Variegated foliage 22
Variegated Liriope 22
Variegated Mondo Grass 22
Verticillium wilt 70
Vines 34
Virginia Stock 30

W

Watering 66, 102
Weed control 45-48
Weigela 34
White flowers 18
White Foxglove 12-13
Wild Indigo 22
Winter tips 56

Y

Yarrow 14
Yellow-edged California Privet . . 22
Yellow foliage 18, 22

Z

Zinnia 26, 28-29, 34, 44
Zonal Geranium 34